Small Talk

Master the Art of Small Talk Easily

(Master the Art of Conversation and Communicate With Confidence)

Bradley Chamblee

Published By **Bella Frost**

Bradley Chamblee

All Rights Reserved

Small Talk: Master the Art of Small Talk Easily (Master the Art of Conversation and Communicate With Confidence)

ISBN 978-0-9953115-7-2

No part of this guidebook shall be reproduced in any form without permission in writing from the publisher except in the case of brief quotations embodied in critical articles or reviews.

Legal & Disclaimer

The information contained in this book is not designed to replace or take the place of any form of medicine or professional medical advice. The information in this book has been provided for educational & entertainment purposes only.

The information contained in this book has been compiled from sources deemed reliable, and it is accurate to the best of the Author's knowledge; however, the Author cannot guarantee its accuracy and validity and cannot be held liable for any errors or omissions. Changes are periodically made to this book. You must consult your doctor or get professional medical advice before using any of the suggested remedies, techniques, or information in this book.

Upon using the information contained in this book, you agree to hold harmless the Author from and against any damages, costs, and expenses, including any legal fees potentially resulting from the application of any of the information provided by this guide. This disclaimer applies to any damages or injury caused by the use and application, whether directly or indirectly, of any advice or information presented, whether for breach of contract, tort, negligence, personal injury, criminal intent, or under any other cause of action.

You agree to accept all risks of using the information presented inside this book. You need to consult a professional medical practitioner in order to ensure you are both able and healthy enough to participate in this program.

Table Of Contents

Chapter 1: Communication Skills, A Necessity.. 1

Chapter 2: How To Talk To Strangers 10

Chapter 3: How To Approach People And Make Friends 34

Chapter 4: How To Initiate First Speak ... 85

Chapter 5: Handle Uncomfortable Pauses Like An Professional. 95

Chapter 6: Conversation Gone Awry (What To Say) 117

Chapter 7: Questions That Make Small Chat Simpler. 134

Chapter 8: The Basics Of Good Conversation... 144

Chapter 9: The Basics Of Bad Conversation 149

Chapter 10: Learn To Listen 155

Chapter 11: Dealing With Awkward Silences... 161

Chapter 12: Starting A Conversation 167

Chapter 13: Ending A Conversation 173

Chapter 14: Fake It Until You Make It .. 179

Chapter 1: Communication Skills, A Necessity

It's never a pleasing sensation when you want to start a communique however don't understand what to begin. That's while small communique is available in!

Small chat is the types of discussion you create when you want to speak to someone however neither of you wants to interact into a particularly deep nor tough topic. Its little" due to the fact you chat about insignificant things, in a manner that fills up silences and helps you each sense extra comfortable and excellent with every different, till you're cushty doing small communicate, permit's look at seven true English small talk topics to get you started out.

Small communicate themes are ideal conversation starters among those who don't know yet another well. If you suffer with social tension disease (SAD), even small chat may be anxiety-upsetting. It might also be difficult if you tend to be greater introverted. Learning to make small speak can also help you the self belief you want to initiate conversations, shape connections, and beef up your social talents. Even if you are uneasy, warding off small chat all absolutely certainly facilitates to irritate anxiety within the long term. Rather of being frightened of small chat, make a point of conquering your fear of it. One useful strategy to ease anxiety is to realize what topics to talk about and what to avoid. Remember that getting to know how to create conversation consists of factors: accuracy and fluency, but conversation is normally extra approximately fluency than it is approximately accuracy, so in case you're going to take part in a discussion with a person, you want to be prepared to concentrate a chunk less on correctness. In other words, you need to put together geared up to make mistakes.

Try to word it on this way: We all have to make errors to expand fluency. Making errors is the fee of admission" for getting more stable in conversation, or remind yourself, I'm going to make mistakes on this dialogue. And that's very well. Improving my speech is worth making mistakes. You may also think about it as a sport of tennis. When you play your first recreation of tennis or volleyball, the first aspect you strive to do is preserve the ball in the air and rancid the floor. But the most effective manner you will progress is if you're ready to drop the ball again and over. Sometimes in dialogue, you're going to drop the ball, and that's all right. You really ought to take it up again.

Do Your Homework" Before a Conversation

There's a motive why human beings call it the artwork" of speakme. It's because verbal exchange is extra than an trade of words. Another purpose why it is able to be so difficult for novices to construct confidence in conversation is because there's a piece of aptitude and craft that goes into it.

Start through analyzing someone proficient in meeting and chatting to new humans. They don't have to speak English, however you need to pay attention to the language they use. How do they have interaction people? How do they preserve the discussion going? Do they ask questions? Do they do most of the speakme? You'll absolutely notice that the only conversationalists ask plenty of observe up questions, and additionally they listen intently.

In an editorial on conversation for the New York Times, Harvard Business professor and researcher Dr. Alison Wood Brooks advocates doing some homework" before chatting to someone new. For example, in case you realize what topics could be captivating in your verbal exchange partner, jot down two or 3 possible thoughts for a dialogue topic, due to the fact here's the fact approximately constructing connections with people in communique:

People enjoy it when you ask them questions.

People revel in it when you speak about topics that interest them.

People experience it while you concentrate to them.

People experience it when you ask them for evaluations or tips.

Being able to have a conversation approximately something clean just like the weather can appear to be it isn't always important, but it's a essential capability to have in case you're mastering a language. Think about how usually you make small chat for your personal language over the day.

Making small chat can also help you:

Avoid uncomfortable silences

Easily get to know someone new

Seem friendlier

Become nearer with colleagues and coworkers

Sound greater like a native speaker

You could make small verbal exchange quite an awful lot whenever you and one (or a few) other people are accrued in a single spot, aren't busy and aren't currently talking about whatever. You can also make small communique at a celebration, before a business assembly or while watching for your meal to microwave inside the place of work. You may also ask someone how his morning become while you're collectively at the elevator, or statement at the weather at the same time as you're waiting for the bus.

Body Language an Important Aspect of Communication

Body Language Is Also a Language, your body communicates nearly as an awful lot as your lips while you communicate and so do the bodies of other human beings. For example, in case you're standing in line to pay for some thing at the shop, and the man or woman in the front of you is grew to become away from you, tapping their foot impatiently and watching at their phone all the time, they possibly don't need to talk to you. If, alternatively, the man or woman in the front of you turns around, catches your eye and grins, you may try initiating a little dialogue.

You may additionally make yourself more reachable by using doing simple things as a way to make a huge impact. If you're attempting to make small chat, or need to suggest which you're engaged in a dialogue, don't go your arms or your legs. Instead, set up eye contact and grin!

Small Talk for Every Occasion

Some issues are accepted, meaning you can use them anywhere and with every person. Others are higher suited for positive eventualities. For example, work-associated themes might be better desirable with colleagues in the administrative center, at the same time as hobby-related ones is probably most popular with pals. Small conversation subjects are small—that is, they're no longer great or vital. Keep it upbeat, and avoid heavy" troubles, especially some thing negative or contentious (a topic many humans disagree on) (a subject many human beings disagree on).

Don't be too random, and wonder the other person with a stunning new difficulty. Let the dialogue unfold organically rather than attempting to ask questions like a listing. The best small talk is the situational range, something you word about your surroundings and integrate into a discussion. For instance, you could tell the fellow you're at the elevator with that the weather is terrible or inquire whether he's searching forward to the weekend (if it's a Friday), however you actually shouldn't ask him what his pursuits are—that's just bizarre! Small talk is a fantastic challenge to examine whether or not you're advanced or just beginning to learn how to keep a communique.

Chapter 2: How To Talk To Strangers

A splendid approach to build up your self belief in starting a verbal exchange is to talk to strangers. And in case you're questioning, But wait! How can I talk to strangers before I actually have good enough confidence?" Here's the aspect: I'm speakme about overall strangers who're inside the equal state of affairs as you. They can also want to enhance their English, or they're without a doubt looking for for other strangers to speak to outdoor of their buddies, family, or the professional surroundings.

So, how will you discover strangers to talk to? If you're willing to be creative, there are dozens of techniques to make it show up

Walking into a room of people used to result in tension for me. I might get so worried, I would communicate in monosyllables (or not at all) feeling tongue-tied, terrified I would say the incorrect element. I could even keep away from eye touch, wishing I should surely listen to human beings and by no means need to end up a part of a dialogue! In my coronary heart I knew this was incorrect. I felt others could look at me as a bland, uninteresting man or woman without a thoughts of my own. I could slip into the background, invisible to human beings around me. I ultimately got here to the factor of doubting whether I ought to even attend gatherings in spite of everything, I changed into really going to move slowly into the nook.

So what turned into the point?

Needless to say, it became obtrusive this technique become NOT effective or serving me well. It wasn't until I finished my executive educate training that I understood conversations may be finished differently. To be sincere, up till this factor, I don't even suppose I had discovered the way to have a communication. For me, this altered the entirety.

When I changed into taking my educate education, I learnt about asking open questions (questions beginning with WHO, WHAT, WHERE, WHEN, WHY or HOW) and began toying with them. I learned that I should inquire approximately some thing if I located 'what' or 'how' in the front of my notion. I learnt that humans definitely need to be visible, heard, and understood. When asked a query, they liked sharing their experiences, know-how, and mind.

I found out that if I asked one open query and then every other, I grew greater calm. This permit me take part inside the debate and at instances, even make a contribution to it. My interest with others in dialogue turned into permitting me to higher apprehend them, and that they me. I changed into able to be greater confident. I even began to sit up for participating in discussions anywhere, every time, about some thing.

Curiosity gave me the self assurance I needed to have conversations with everyone – and you could, too. These 3 strategies will make you confidence to chat to human beings

1. Be found in all talks to ABSORB.

I turned into so preoccupied and worried what others were questioning that I wasn't capable of be present and absolutely pay attention to what turned into being stated. This made it difficult for me to be an active player or a assured conversationalist. As soon as I become capable of be gift and simply concentrate to ABSORB what became being said, I discovered it SO a lot less difficult to be fascinated. This additionally helped me feel greater confident, when you consider that being there supposed I understood exactly what turned into being said. ABSORB is an acronym. See below:

A: Attention to others. If we aren't giving the speaker our entire interest, we aren't absolutely present and will by no means be able to actively listen to what's being stated.

B: Body language and tone of voice. It is important to look at the speaker's frame language and tone of voice, as well as your very own. Where are you searching? What are your arms doing? Are your words congruent along with your frame language and tone of voice? It is critical to understand of the message you're expressing to the speaker — lively listening doesn't only entail words.

S: Stop and concentrate. This means placed your smartphone aside, shut your ebook or mag, or pass far from your pc. This permits you to give the speaker your entire interest!

O: Open to knowledge, NOT judgment. It is not possible to be fascinated and find out about people if we condemn them or anticipate we recognise what's excellent for them. We all have our own wonderful evaluations, attitude, and experiences. We can examine loads from each different, if we're open to information in place of criticizing people. As you interact discussions, try to maintain your attention on the speaker and be involved as you learn about them. This is set them, NOT you.

R: Repeat through paraphrasing. This is an first-rate method to assure that you draw close what the speaker is saying. It helps you to be on the same web page. When we aren't on the identical web page, a number of assumptions are made, judgements are handed, and talks get complicated which results in warfare. Paraphrasing is likewise a extraordinary approach to suggest to the speaker: 'I hear you, I see you, I understand you' on this moment, in preference to mending or solving some thing for them that turned into unsolicited.

You realize what I am speaking about. When someone involves you and complains, you want to assist via making things higher and propose them what to do. DON'T. Paraphrase as an alternative.

B: Be calm amid your gremlins. The gremlins are those troublesome voices in a single's mind. We all have them. They may be a ticker tape of to-do lists, critique others, and/or struggle with our capability to fully concentrate. By deliberately being privy to them, you are able to turn down the ones voices and give the speaker your whole attention to ABSORB what's being said.

Tip: Remembering to enroll in each discussion and ABSORB what the speaker is announcing (as opposed to every and each thing) allow you to continue to be gift and targeted at the speaker to peer, hear, and recognize them. This by myself will assist you be greater confident and generate an impact with anyone you speak with.

2. Choose to concentrate in a way that makes a speciality of the speaker at the

same time as maintaining open and non-judging.

You can be thinking, Choose a way to listen? We either concentrate or we don't, right?" Sort of. While selecting NOT to pay attention is truly an option, I think there are extra alternatives you constantly have whilst listening. How we pick out to pay attention affects how we technique the facts we're receiving. So, we may additionally choose to investigate the statistics via our very own lens, ideas, and studies and choose/examine the speaker based on our personal stories. In your mind, this decision appears like I think you …., I want you to.., I want you to…" This fashion of listening puts your internal emphasis on self instead of on the other person. This choice doesn't supply a variety of opportunity for studying or inquiry. It is limiting, considering that we anticipate we understand what is high-quality based totally on our views and reports.

Next, we may additionally opt to maintain the highlight on YOU. In this option, we evaluate the facts and verify the speaker in the speaker's own context. This feels like supporting" or fixing and solving". We trust we are helping and repairing and solving while we're in reality judging. This sounds like You must..., you need to..., you could't.." This decision is likewise restrictive seeing that we count on we're concentrating at the speaker by way of helping them with out expertise anything about what goes on for them or what they want to accomplish.

Another desire is choosing to concentrate with expertise. In this alternative, we choose to hold the attention at the speaker. We droop all judgment and are completely open. This is NOT about us this is approximately them. And the most effective aspect to do is concentrate and be inquisitive to examine from them. This alternative feels like what are you going to do? How are you...? When can you..." When we suspend our judgment and remain open and fascinated, possibilities and possibilities come to be on hand that in any other case wouldn't. This is how we cooperate and innovate — connecting and mastering from others. This is how we've got better talks: interactions wherein we feel assured.

Finally, there are times if you have pores and skin in the game and you have a vested stake within the result. There is a threat to be fascinated to study, even as additionally pleasing your demands in the conclusion. So this appears like We need to depart via 5 pm. What do you need from me so we will depart on time?" OR I actually have every other meeting in an hour. How can we layout this assembly so we get what is required achieved before I need to go away?"

How you choose to listen will without delay determine the nice of your discussion and its end. It is vital to spotlight that there is a time and vicinity for every choice of listening. I observed that choosing to pay attention on others and understanding others helped me be extra confident. What additionally gave me self assurance changed into spotting that I ALWAYS had a preference.

3. Ask open inquiring inquiries to better realise the reviews of others.

The quickest and simplest technique to be more confident and keep a better communication is to transfer the eye from one's self to any other person. This may be carried out through asking open inquiries, queries that begin with who, what, wherein, when, and the way.

We might also on occasion hold judgment, specially when emotion is concerned, so be extraordinarily cautious. An intriguing remark is that now not many individuals have a number of experience asking open questions, for this reason they generally sense uneasy asking them. However, with repetition, they emerge as second nature.

If you locate your self grappling with an open question, definitely insert a what" or how" in the front of your belief. If you get definitely stuck, inform me more" is also a wonderful technique to preserve the discussion open, involved and confident.

With the traits in era, appropriate exceptional, assured interactions have become more difficult to behavior. We all have less exercise, much less time, much less concentration, less self belief. The exceptional component is, curiosity gives us greater of the whole thing. It fills us up. It is how we learn, have interaction, engage, explore, inspire and extraordinarily enough, it additionally makes us blissful. When we are interested in humans, we experience extraordinary. This emotion facilitates us stay calm in talks with others. When we are fascinated and ask questions, there's a mind/ heart connection. Dopamine and oxytocin are launched; brain chemical substances that make us experience happy. This implies that, with inquiring talks, we experience greater stable and related to human beings – even in confrontation. It doesn't get a great deal better than that.

Do you recollect the closing time you stood in front of an target audience to speak?

You remembered the whole thing you wanted to mention, but you have been anxious, and maybe your voice was wobbly at the outset. Afterwards, you searched the room to peer whether or not all people favored your talk, hoping for feedback from the faces round. Your organization makes eye contact and also you wish he didn't understand how concerned you have been. Does this sound such as you? Maybe you have been within the equal scenario not long

What is confidence?

Confidence is recognizing the value you deliver and behaving in a way that shows it to different people.

Why must I fear approximately self belief?

Believe in your self! Have agree with for your capability! Without a modest however affordable accept as true with for your personal competencies you can't be successful or glad." Having a great feeling of self assurance is a motivation whilst you are mastering English. Confidence in our capabilities and our ability motivates us to push ourselves greater. Studies propose that strengthening your self belief also can assist you at paintings. Confidence in your very own competencies at work will suggest that your manager may have greater self belief in your skills, which might cause multiplied obligations at work. When you are assured to your abilities you're more open to studying opportunities, consisting of expert development lessons at your organization, no longer simplest that, but in case you are chargeable for interacting with clients, your self belief will lead them to believe you greater.

Now which you recognize why you need to trust whilst carrying out a communique, permit's explore eight approaches to assist you higher.

1. Master fluency

Part of being confident is speaking successfully. If you speak properly and loudly, you will seem and experience extra assured. A fundamental method in an effort to help is gaining knowledge of to study with fluency.

What does it suggest? It implies which you exercise studying a bit of literature so you appear confident now not just in what you say, but the way you say it.

Some guidelines to get you commenced:

Start with analyzing content you are already acquainted with, including something out of your lesson or a piece of literature you've study previously, examine it aloud in front of a reflect. Notice what your body language is like. Are you standing up directly or hunching over? Speaking loudly, or quietly? Work on adjusting how you stand and how you speak (your body language has a exceptionally huge impact in your confidence, which we'll look extra at later), utilize the equal text until you don't forget it, and you may now begin that specialize in the way you speak for your target market. If you want to degree your progress, video your self reading the material the primary time, and alternatively after you don't forget it. Seeing those tendencies can assist to in addition enhance your self assurance. Go beforehand and exercise with a trusted buddy when you sense extra snug.

2. Mimic English TV information presenters

If you're now not positive the way to behave optimistically, a tremendous option is to have a look at human beings. You need if you want to grasp what they do that makes them so assured. There's no higher manner to recognise this than with the aid of looking at the ones who've to talk in front of hundreds of thousands of people each day — news newshounds and broadcasters. While it is able to be tempting to watch the news in your own language, it's far exceptional to watch it in English.

First, you get to exercising your listening talents. Second, you need with a purpose to emulate their tone and pronunciation so that you can do the equal in English. If you don't believe you could accomplish this, actually consider that even local English speakers have a hard time speakme in the front of an target audience. Those newscasters can do that because they have skilled for endless hours over a few years. You, too, may be as confident as them — however you want to put inside the time and paintings.

To get commenced, choose one information application to watch regular. It facilitates in case you pick simply one man or woman you like. For instance, try the BBC One-minute international information.

Here are some matters to ask your self while you watch the motion pictures:

How do they take a seat?

What is the tone in their voice like?

How rapidly do they talk?

Finally, pick a video. Watch it, then watch it once more. After viewing it a few times, it's time to replicate what the news reporter says. Speak concurrently with the reporter until you feel snug saying it while not having to view the video, then strive once more with some other one.

three. Understand your frame language

There is a lot of studies concerning the energy of frame language and its impact on how different humans view you, and also how we see ourselves.

four. Share your problems with someone you accept as true with

Sometimes all we want to sense better approximately discussion is understanding that we're not the best person who suffers, and that others also battle with positive things, inclusive of how they appear even as speaking to their employer. Go in advance and speak your problems with a close pal, your partner, a instructor, or maybe a straightforward co-employee. This isn't always approximately whining. Rather, it's a time to explicit what you don't experience self belief in, or what you're managing, don't criticize your self or remember why you don't feel confident, in an effort to not help. Instead, say what you have got to say, and flow on. Sometimes, letting our anger out is all we need to feel better. That way we will cross again to refining our talking capabilities.

five. Prepare communication openers

It may be tension wracking even as attending to networking activities or truly interacting with co-workers that have advanced communique capability than you. In this state of affairs, it might help if you put together at the least 10 sentences to serve as verbal exchange openers. That way you're now not standing about with uncomfortable silences which could simply make you extra uneasy and much less assured, you could put together communication starters for severa instances. So, regardless of wherein you are, you may be prepared for any circumstance.

6. Work on addressing difficulties in businesses

Part of being confident calls for realizing that different individuals may be struggling with with the identical demanding situations. Studies show that once we apprehend this, it allows with our vanity, and in flip with our self belief, on this have a look at teachers found that they are able to help students benefit confidence by encouraging them to mirror on beyond lessons, and how important it become to share their struggles with teachers and students alike. It's crucial to work with a person you agree with — in case you don't feel comfortable speakme about your problems, then how will you restoration them?

It is helpful to talk to trusted colleagues, or perhaps join a mastermind group in your neighborhood place – a mastermind group is certainly a set of specialists who meet collectively to speak about a subject of their desire, for your case, improving your confidence, those are informal agencies which can be prepared with the aid of their individuals, created to help each other research and exchange thoughts, or just to community. There aren't any formal corporations to enroll in up for, but you may try collecting a group of individuals together, such as your paintings colleagues, a neighborhood social group, or maybe fellow professionals from a forum or LinkedIn group you engage in.

7. Read fulfillment tales about individuals who've high conversation capacity

We all every so often need a bit encouragement, and I'd advise you to study approximately those who have correctly perfected the act of conversation, studying approximately how others have been successful enables to encourage a fantastic technique. These achievement tales will also assist you understand what methods they have utilized to gain greater self assurance, changed into it due to the fact they believed in themselves? Or turned into it because they practiced a lot? Make a few notes and seek advice from them again later while you are analyzing.

eight. Reflect for your achievements

Reflecting on what you have got achieved to date will assist you recognise how plenty you've actually positioned. It is also a confidence improve as it demonstrates precisely how difficult you've labored.

Here are a few tips:

Keep a notebook or a studying log in which you write down each day what you worked on or finished

Create a survey/remarks shape to offer your self unique feedback to your competencies (make sure you query individuals who've greater communication ability than you) (make certain you ask human beings who have higher communication skills than you). If you are taking a path, chat for your trainer regularly and ask what they determined about your development. Start thinking at your errors as chances to have a study.

Remember that, clearly as you have got got conquered other hurdles in your existence, you could furthermore conquer this!

Chapter 3: How To Approach People And Make Friends

I've continually been timid and introverted, so it's quite hard for me to in truth pass as much as a person and begin a conversation. I currently relocated to a brand new place, and I want to recognize how to technique people with out being weird so I can set up friends. Any guidelines?" If you aren't typically outgoing, it might be difficult to talk to human beings and recognise a manner to method them. With someone you don't comprehend, it's everyday to enjoy nervous and on your thoughts to begin considering everything that may work incorrect like: 'I'll certainly say some element silly' or 'I'm so awkward.' Unchecked, thoughts like the ones may probably encourage you to keep away from social contacts and reaffirm your awful views, even though they aren't actual. While you can agree with that you are clearly uncomfortable or have horrific social talents, it's greater possibly which you are preventing with social tension. According to have a examine, 90% of individuals will have an episode of social tension for the duration of their life, so if you experience involved around others, you clearly aren't by myself. The right statistics is that social tension doesn't should imply spending your lifestyles in exile without having the potential to speak to others or set up buddies.

In reality, maximum human beings may additionally additionally triumph over their social anxiety with the resource of venturing out of their consolation zone, assembly others, and having greater discussions. Research indicates that having greater social connections is healthful for you in lots of strategies. More encounters may also additionally help decorate your social talents, your self notion, and your fashionable first-rate of existence, even when those chats are shallow. With the ones primary verbal exchange starters and drawing close strategies, you will be better organized to fulfill human beings and make pals at meetings, activities, at art work, or perhaps in public. Below are strategies which assist you to method people, initiate discussions, and increase your social competencies, at the equal time as additionally growing more confident in your self.

1. Use a pleasing welcome

A excellent welcome goes an extended way toward generating a high-quality first influence. Because maximum people conflict with some diploma of social tension, being super allows others loosen up and experience extra comfortable beginning as a lot as you. Being great moreover permits to make you more available, so you received't always need to be the best to approach them in the future. The finest approach to welcome a person in individual is to smile, greet them pleasantly, and inquire how their day is going. If you're beginning your chat on line, the usage of exclamation elements and emoji is a smart approach to provide a nice mood. A extremely good welcome is a fail secure method to create a pleasant tone for a talk and also will make subsequent conversations a good deal much less complicated to technique.

2. Introduce your self

It may additionally moreover seem apparent, but introducing oneself is a critical first step in coming near human beings. If you have got anxiety, the greater you wait, the more worry should in all likelihood upward thrust, and the tougher it is able to be to introduce oneself. Because introductions are supposed to return again first, delaying to introduce oneself also can make it less snug for others to talk to you. Whether it's your first day at artwork or you are getting into a assembly or birthday celebration, get introductions out of the way faster in place of later. Walk up, introduce yourself, and deliver a sturdy (but now not too business enterprise) handshake. When it's their time, attempt to announce their name earlier than departing the come upon. This will help you maintain in mind it and is also a hooked up technique to create a excellent effect.

3. Lean in and get near

Trying to introduce oneself at some level in the room may additionally additionally make matters unpleasant, even as fame too a long way makes it now not viable to speak and sends unfriendly signs to others. Try to get near sufficient to shake their hand or pay hobby them talk in a low voice, but no longer so near that you may lean beforehand and warfare heads with them. By following this guiding principle, you can get within the route of people with out appearing creepy or ordinary. If you're questioning the way to technique a modern organization of humans, the correct manner to include oneself is to set up your self into the institution. Avoid dispositions to sit down down outdoor of a circle or in the route of the rear of the room. This will make it hard to talk with others and additionally sends delinquent signs and symptoms that you want to be left by myself. Instead, discover a seat close to to someone and lean in the direction of them on the identical time as they talk to you. This will propose which you want to be worried and could make it less difficult for humans to technique you.

4. Ask a query

Asking questions is a few different extremely good method to approach someone and may be an easy in" to introduce oneself and is a easy manner to start small chat. For instance, if it's your first day at the interest, you possibly have plenty of questions, and most humans may be thrilled to assist you. You want to select out the precise opportunity to invite a query, so don't approach a person in the event that they appearance busy or worrying. Instead, wait till they're to be had after which technique them. If you are wondering the manner to method a person you need to be friends with, asking questions is also a tested strategy to illustrate hobby and create an excellent have an effect on. [4] For example, asking a person what they revel in about their art work, what they do of their entertainment time, or whether or not or not they've seen any super programs are powerful approaches to start discussions. Questions like the ones furthermore help you discover some element in common with people, that is what quantity of friendships begin.

five. Comment on a few issue that stands out

After assembly humans and introducing oneself, the subsequent diploma is to discover strategies to provoke discussions. When you're worried, your mind may moreover need to transport easy, race, or begin overthinking what you need to say.

Making observations on matters spherical you'll be a fantastic manner to begin a communication organically and can also assist you get out of your mind even because it isn't helping you discover topics to speak about. Look spherical you to discover whatever that stands proud, then make use of this to kick off a communicate. For instance, you could factor out an thrilling photo, the climate, or reward a person on some thing they're wearing. Avoid being harsh or judgemental of others whilst making observations considering the fact that this might make others fearful of you. Instead, statement on devices on your environment which might be exciting, uncommon, or which you appreciate.

6. Pretend you're already friends

When you have a whole lot of fear in advance than talking to someone, your mind would possibly begin cataloging all of the topics that could bypass incorrect during the interaction. You may want to worry that you will be uncomfortable or say a few thing bizarre. These thoughts can also furthermore feed into your fear, and additionally they maintain you overly targeted on fending off pronouncing the incorrect factor, which can also force you to live mute. Changing your perspective via way of believing that strangers are pals you haven't met may possibly make it lots much less tough to technique human beings. Imagine your closest pal changed into there, instead of the stranger in front of you. What might you are saying to them? This technique allows you to regulate your wondering, anticipate extra really, and makes it less difficult to attach in a herbal and normal way.

7. Find a similar venture

Empathy builds intimacy in relationships, permitting individuals to attach via similar reports. Finding a not unusual hassle can also furthermore produce this empathy and is an high-quality approach to proper away installation rapport with someone. Avoid oversharing or diving into your darkest traumas and fears with a person you really met, and alternatively deal with ordinary troubles you can moderately presume they connect to. For instance, if you spot a colleague racing into the place of work, ask them whether they encountered the equal web site visitors jam you have been behind schedule in, or if it's bloodless outdoor, make a comic tale approximately it. By connecting via a comparable trouble, you may be capable of enlarge a dating with someone, even if you don't apprehend them very well.

8. Make a private remark

People like being singled out, as long as you do it in an exceptional manner. For instance, supply a observation regarding someone's domestic or their meals at the same time as you are invited to a party at their vicinity. Be honest, and don't overdo this technique due to the truth turning in too many praises should probable make others uncomfortable and skeptical of you. Be watchful to important human beings and be aware of statistics. This indicates interest in them and may help you create a super first effect. Showing interest in precise human beings also permits you be an awful lot less focused on yourself, it's far a win-win for individuals who discover it tough to talk to others due to self-interest or social anxiety.

nine. Use first-rate frame language

Communication includes more than truely the terms you communicate. Your frame language consists of your facial emotions, gestures, and posture. It's a critical a part of conversation. Positive frame language draws extraordinary human beings to you and includes developing terrific eye contact, leaning in, and maintaining an open stance. Because many people battle with social tension, proper frame language facilitates you look greater warmness and to be had. Using actual body language makes other people enjoy cushty drawing close to you, chatting to you, and commencing as heaps as you.

10. Show exhilaration

When humans are pleased, it seems in their speech and their frame language. They will be inclined to use their hands extra after they speak, located greater emphasis to their sentences, and utilize more facial expressions. Enthusiasm pulls others to you, making them involved and worried in what you have got to say. Hand symptoms can also be used to wave howdy to a person for the duration of the room or to capture someone's interest. In a set of humans, elevating a finger or a hand can also be a clever technique to ask for a risk to talk without interrupting.

eleven. Send and observe welcoming signs and symptoms

Whether you are trying to technique one person or a fixed of human beings, it would advantage to understand a manner to interpret social signs and signs. Specifically, looking for welcoming warning symptoms may also additionally assist you ensure your technique is properly-timed and properly-received. Avoid drawing near a person after they look concerned, harried, or busy, due to the fact you may be interrupting them or catching them at a horrible moment. Also, make certain to offer welcoming signs to different humans with the resource of giving them your whole hobby, smiling, nodding, and asking questions. This suggests that you're interested in them and is a verified approach to create a splendid affect. People who can choose up on those warning signs and symptoms and signs and symptoms may additionally revel in extra snug coming near you, which means you received't need to do all the effort.

12. Take turns talking

When you're attending a meeting, birthday party, or meeting, you may arrive right right into a speak this is already taking region, and you can need to expect a lull earlier than welcoming others. This is the exception to the norm of introducing oneself early considering the reality that it's miles courteous to interrupt. When there may be a pause, you may revel in unfastened to join in, welcome mother and father, introduce your self, and take a turn.

When you're worried, you can will be inclined of both speakme an excessive amount of or no longer saying enough. While you don't want to take too many rounds, you furthermore may additionally don't want to avoid taking turns to speak. Not chatting enough stops others from analyzing you and gives fewer opportunities to connect.

13. Play communicate Jenga

Another method to approach a speak is to consider it as it's miles a recreation of Jenga, wherein every participant takes turns constructing on what the previous individual stated. Instead of feeling including you need to persuade or initiate each communicate, remember drawing lower back and discover ways to enlarge on what high-quality human beings say. Building on an ongoing communicate is a terrific technique to include oneself without interrupting or taking manipulate. This offers human beings the ability to maintain the problem in areas they choice, making it more likely they may be inquisitive about the communication. Following the herbal go with the flow of a conversation also gets rid of the load off of you to constantly feel the need to influence and might assist make talks appear less forced.

14. Find strategies to beneficial useful useful resource

Helping distinctive humans, even in tiny approaches, is every other awesome method to technique people in a pleasant manner. Notice whilst a person looks as if they're having problems with some component and provide to provide them a hand. For example, if you are at a party and the host seems aggravating, provide to help in with the set-up or clean-up. The change of favors is likewise a extremely good method to create receive as proper with with human beings and encourage them to like you. By supplying to help, you're telling them that you are listening to them and furthermore that you want to be useful. Because that may be a feature most human beings search for in a chum, it might be a incredible approach to construct a reference to someone.

15. Adopt a curious mentality

When you sense uneasy or awkward, you are normally locked in the important part of your mind, overthinking everything you do and say and being too focused on your self. Curiosity is a superb shortcut to get out of this location of your thoughts and to achieve a mentality that is lot more snug, open, and adaptable. This open mentality is one in which you're a protracted way more likely to have encounters which may be herbal, free-flowing, and honest. A inquisitive mentality is one that is open and shows a state of mindfulness, which has regarded to lower tension and help human beings emerge as greater gift and involved in the proper here-and-now. Mindfulness makes it less difficult to speak in techniques that appear herbal and will assist you pay attention greater on others than yourself, this is one of the outstanding strategies to narrate, be part of, and inspire others to like you.

Final thoughts

When you don't realise someone well, it might be awkward or maybe intimidating to approach them and start a speak. It's essential to do not forget that most humans are remarkable, and are demanding to meet humans, have good sized discussions, and installation buddies. Keeping this in thoughts will make it less difficult to technique humans and discover techniques to hook up with them.

Also, thinking about practically anybody battles with their very very own doubts and social anxiety, taking the initiative in coming close to individuals may also even reduce their anxiety. Using those strategies will not first-rate make it less complex to approach humans, but they may also make it more likely that first-rate people will experience comfortable drawing near you.

There are massive techniques to growing communication you can make use of. You may additionally moreover have seen them covered some vicinity else. Having a commonplace technique can be rather beneficial due to the fact:

It provides you a free trendy method or activity plan to conform with. You have a number one idea of what you want to carry out and in which the communicate is headed. You do no longer have to suppose as lots, and it frees up your mind to pay attention on being attentive to the opportunity individual or bobbing up with the following factor you need to say.

It would possibly possibly enhance your feeling of self guarantee and luxury. You apprehend you're the usage of an technique that is worked previously. You're now not surely flying with the useful resource of the seat of your trousers.

It is probably a pleasing, easy vicinity to start for going to be had to exercising more. Rather of thinking, "I haven't any clue how to speak to humans", you have were given a preferred gadget you may strive out.

That said, no ordinary method to growing verbal exchange is going to provide you a really perfect method to get alongside component all and sundry you come across. It's in no way that honest. However, the use of one is lots higher than moving into genuinely unprepared. Also, there may be not anything saying you could not have a few wonderful techniques equipped to move, and if one doesn't paintings, you can try each other. You may additionally moreover even switch up sizable techniques inner a unmarried speak because it progresses. You do no longer need to firmly try to use certainly one method to all and sundry or state of affairs. Here they are:

Be concerned about unique human beings and make it your goal to discover what's thrilling and first-rate about them

This is the most normal desired approach you could concentrate folks describe. It indicates up time and again in all types of places. The idea right here is which you're generally going to be a question asker and a listener and pay hobby the communique on the opportunity person. Your "motive" within the chat is to find out what makes people charming.

The essential idea about why this technique works is that everyone's preferred difficulty count number is themselves, and they will revel in someone who takes a real hobby in them and the topics they've got to say. People moreover have a tendency to feel good about a discussion if they're afforded an area to speak about factors of themselves that they're pleased with and obsessed with (e.G., they get to joyfully inform a person how loads they driven themselves with the resource of visiting for the duration of South America on a modest fee variety) (e.G., they get to excitedly inform someone how lots they driven themselves by using way of traveling around South America on a tiny charge range). Another cliché you could listen frequently almost about this approach is that you may be lot extra effective taking an interest in wonderful human beings than you may via seeking to cause them to interested by you.

A advantage of this method is that it predisposes you to adopt a pleasing, welcoming united states of america of mind. Its primary idea says that everyone is well well worth talking to in case you go beneath some issue superficial prejudices you may have about them. And because of the reality you are in all likelihood to honestly find out a few component intriguing, it sooner or later sooner or later ends up becoming a self-enjoyable prophesy. This is probably perfect for folks whose default setting is to be a bit horrible about others. A second fantastic is that it gets rid of the weight off you to try to win everybody over via manner of being first rate-colourful and attractive.

When making use of this technique you do no longer want to actually be interviewing the opportunity individual or speakme approximately them the whole time. You can even though deliver up things about yourself and percentage your personal reviews at the same time as it is relevant to accomplish that. However, the overall emphasis of the talk is on them.

Talk in phrases of the opposite person's hobbies

This technique is pretty similar to the most effective in advance than, in which you're in big factor listening and the speak is constructed spherical them and the subjects they decide upon discussing. The assumptions about why it absolutely works are just like well. I nearly grouped them all beneath one name.

They're not exactly the equal but. The method above is more popular, and is set coming across human beings's extraordinary attributes, a few factor they may be. This one is more about deliberately looking for out what someone is interested by speakme about, and focussing the speak on that. You take an hobby in their hobby and ask questions about it, otherwise you concentrate and permit them to can help you understand about it. They might also moreover need to speak approximately a interest of theirs, or perhaps they may need to inform someone approximately their up-and-down dating with their sister. Whatever it's far, go along with it.

I be given as authentic with every of these listening/distinctive character-centric techniques may work absolutely correctly. However, on the equal time I take shipping of as real with their usefulness might be a hint over-hyped. That's no longer to suggest they may be worthless. They're certainly the not nice, one-length-fits-all strategies they will be often touted as. I speak about their limits further in this article:

Listening and Being Interested In People Isn't a Conversation Cure-All, it additionally discusses the way to keep away from uncomfortable silence, trap wonderful buddies, and why you do not need a "interesting lifestyles" to generate fascinating verbal exchange. Click right here to retain to the free schooling.

Try to the touch on a topic you each obviously like to talk approximately

It's pretty easy to assume of things to say whilst you're talking approximately some issue you're genuinely interested by. Like if someone likes movies, some thing as easy because the phrase "Martin Scorcese" can also spark a dozen thoughts and perspectives and ability speak topics to pop of their mind. Likewise, in case you're chatting to a person, and you each actually need to talk approximately the same problem, the talk will in all likelihood to flow extremely manifestly. Everything you are saying to each super will spark a number of sparkling matters you can probably supply up. Odds are more you may furthermore connect to and like them, because they'll be into the same matters that you are. This technique is ready trying to get that shape of discourse going.

To start out with this method you first ought to discover if there are any belongings you every desire to talk about about. You may additionally additionally accomplish this by means of the usage of using asking them approximately their pursuits "So what sort of sports activities activities do you do for fun?", "Do you put together dinner loads?", and so forth. You can also make feedback on problems which might be thrilling to you, and preference they generate a debate, e.G., "Wow, you must have visible the game final night." The fundamental getting-to-apprehend-you small chat that usually opens a communicate once in a while serves this purpose of trying to find a few commonplace floor.

Figure out what subjects you've got were given were given an smooth, amusing time speaking approximately, and then try to lead the dialogue in that manner

Again, this approach has masses in common with the fine in advance than it. Here the focal point is a bit much less on fishing round locating a together exciting scenario, and more on beginning with what you need to talk and trying to form the speak round your consolation place. Though for it to paintings you every want, a) for the alternative person to need to speak about the hassle as nicely, or b) to discover a person who does no longer mind taking note of you bypass on about it (probably they are the use of one of the first techniques).

This is seemed extra of a selfish tactic, as you're looking for to guide the concern to topics you want to talk approximately. It's regularly taken into consideration of as more form to pay attention on the other character. However, I though embody it for the purpose that it's miles a primary concept that can help someone put together their mind and simplify how they method an engagement. I furthermore do not forget in proper doses it's miles honestly

OK to try to talk about the topics you're enthusiastic about. You handiest should be conscious to particular people and take care now not to bore them or dominate the air region.

Try to get the alternative man or woman interested in and stimulated with the useful useful resource of you

This may probably take a number of paperwork, which include:

Discussing your skills and successes

Joking about and essentially trying to illustrate how hilarious you're

Making remarks that preferably replicate how informed and perceptive you are

This technique in reality has a more terrible which means that. There's more of a disadvantage if you attempt to comply with it and it does not strike the target. You might be perceived as insecure and attempting too hard, or as a person who's self-absorbed and complete of themselves. It additionally flies in the face of the "It's higher to be interested by other human beings than strive to steer them to be into you" notion implicit in the techniques referred to previously.

The reason is that it's OK to cognizance on our outstanding elements, however they need to come out organically, not because of the fact we are looking for to cram them into the talk. Again, the motive I convey it up at all is due to the fact it is but a hobby plan some people adopt. I'm additionally going to be honest and say all of us lapse into this tactic sometimes, whether or not or no longer or no longer we're aware about it or not, specially while we're speaking to a person we surely do want to affect or win over. I hold in mind in very cautious moderation could be very well, and that there can be no longer whatever too wrong with looking to put your fantastic foot in advance or bring hobby for your skills. Of route, you need to be sensitive and cautious within the way you do it.

First and critical, if you want to approach individuals and set up friends correctly, you'll first want to be presentable. Be presentable enough which you appear trustworthy with out being overly threatening. As lousy as it sounds, it is herbal for max humans to just accept as right with individuals who appear presentable. Those that appear to be they have got their existence on top of things. You need to appear to be that in case you need to method humans and make friends.

All you need to do is be tidy. Be sanitary and make certain your clothing aren't frayed, scruffy, and wrinkles. Pick a get dressed fashion that suits you and stay with it. If this is a component you're now not too acquainted with, gather steerage from a chum or a representative. Trim your nail, easy your hair, heady scent exceptional, the works.

You don't want to seem appealing for the purpose of being cute, you actually need to do the individuals you're going to be going as a good buy because the courtesy of being presentable. On top of that, humans will sense greater cushty being approached with the aid of manner of someone who's presentable than someone who's now not.

Read the room

Before drawing near a person at a party, at artwork, or anywhere it's far you are, ensure the person you're drawing near doesn't mind being approached. There are people who have an excessive amount of on their mind, are looking for a person, or just really need to be left on my own. Whatever their motivations are, you shouldn't pry.

The idea is, there can be people who received't mind being contacted. In fact, masses of humans embody it. What you need to do now might be to recognize such oldsters so you can also furthermore approach people who are open instead of having rejected outright.

Most folks that don't want to be contacted will sincerely brazenly permit you to understand. Some of them will in truth stand there, smile, and be courteous. When in reality, they'd determine upon be left on my own. When you meet the ones parents, in reality be terrific and say your good-bye. Before drawing close to them, folks who don't want to be disturbed will typically stiffen up and divert their eyes.

Focus on people who appearance first rate about being contacted. They'll act hopeful or maybe gaze at you as you method. In time, you'll develop higher at detecting those folks. For now, maintain a similarly eye out at the same time as studying the room.

Introduce your self effectively. Once you eventually approach someone, the subsequent step is to introduce your self as it ought to be. Make high quality you're capable of speak yourself and the man or woman you're speaking to can pay hobby you loud and smooth. If this is a few element you're no longer acquainted with, you may need to workout this at domestic, in the the front of a mirror. It can also additionally appear and appear silly, but that could be a form of workout you'll want to adopt.

When coming near a person, you don't even want to give them your call without delay. You may want to possibly begin with small communication or some aspect inside the room that ought to be spoken about. Once you feel the alternative man or woman is up for interplay, that's even as you may introduce yourself. You may also moreover additionally truly supply out your name while extending your hand for a handshake. That's all you want to do. Be fantastic your voice is crisp and your handshake is powerful.

Don't be too guarded

If your purpose is to technique humans and set up pals, being excessively guarded is the opportunity of the component you want to carry out. If you're someone who's acquainted with being reserved and personal, you can need to get used to the idea of opening up now for the purpose of socializing.

You don't want to reveal everything approximately yourself. You surely want to be cushty with the notion of starting up your self as tons as exclusive humans to any amount further. You'll need to percentage your aspirations and desires in life. Your hobbies. The topics that thrill you and those that grind your gears. You'll want to speak to different human beings along with you're speakme to a chum. Whenever you're requested a query about your self, don't be shy of setting out your self. This is one method you could create pals, in the long run. Just workout doing this from right here on out. You may additionally discover the activity pretty calming.

Mind the distance among you and the alternative person

When talking to a person, make sure there's a terrific hole most of the of you. You want to be near enough so interactions are smooth and intelligible, and definitely so the possibility man or woman can enjoy and recognize which you're interested in getting to know them higher, but no longer so close to that it's already invasive, simply thoughts the space among you and the alternative man or woman. Get near enough, but now not too near, don't be too a long way off both. You want them to experience which you're being engaged with them.

Be interested in the person you're speaking to

This is an hobby you may adopt going earlier if you want so you can approach human beings and set up friends. Force your thoughts to be involved approximately the individual you're speaking to, or the man or woman you need to talk to. Let that hobby make bigger up. Put precise mind to your head together with, I marvel what this man or woman is like" or I marvel what this person's hopes and objectives are." Once you've positioned the ones mind into your brain, you can then push your self to meet your interest with the beneficial aid of really strolling as a notable deal as that person and analyzing them.

This is an exercise you can stress yourself to do pretty resultseasily. It's a few element you'll need to intentionally do early on, but with sufficient repetition, that is a few element in order to start coming naturally to you. Every time you meet someone you want to speak to, your interest will already blossom, so as to make you need to speak to that man or woman more due to the fact you'll be so anxious to meet your interest.

Don't be terrified of factors going incorrect

One of the belongings you definitely shouldn't do in case you need to technique people and installation pals is being terrified of factors going incorrect. If you allow this form of dread to take manipulate, you'll in no manner be able to carry out a few difficulty correctly.

Don't be involved of things going incorrect socially. You're without a doubt entitled for your errors. When it does come, research to feel good about it and circulate on. Don't be afraid of a few detail earlier than it even passed off. Although that is completely normal, it's a few component you'll need to regularly discover ways to save you doing if you want to method humans and set up friends.

Force your thoughts to suppose every body you're coming near is already a pal

This is each different smart approach you could make use of so you don't come to be too worried to technique a person.

Whenever you word a person you want to technique however are too frightened to carry out that, push your mind into believing that that individual is already your pal. You wouldn't feel uneasy coming near a chum, would likely you?

It's going to be difficult earlier than the whole lot, but the greater you push yourself to think accordingly, the more in reality it's going to emerge as subsequently. Plus, now not simplest will this assist you genuinely method someone however it'll additionally help you be nicer with them at some level inside the engagement.

Don't be scared of small speak, however don't use them too much every

Small chats can also every make or damage a conversation. There's now not something essentially wrong with them, of path, but if a person uses small communicate too regularly even as attempting to get to apprehend someone, they proper away make that speak stale.

That said, use it sparingly. It's quality to touch upon matters together with the web web page site visitors or the weather for as prolonged as it's relevant and profitable to talk about. However, you need to ultimately bypass on to making the communique greater significant. Don't get caught on merely utilizing small communication. Start to genuinely get to recognize the opportunity character.

Find a common ground

Once you've engaged a person in a communication, the following step that may be a hurdle for you is to hold the communication. Not satisfactory keep it but certainly make it big. Approaching a person is one component, but turning into buddies with them is a whole new special sport. One of the techniques you would in all likelihood advantage this is through the usage of identifying a not unusual floor among you and the opposite character. Start asking them about their pursuits and percent yours as well. As you keep speakme, you can in all likelihood find out an interest you both share. That also can then be the gravity of your discourse going ahead. This will permit you to construct a relationship with the opportunity person.

Be observant

Being watchful is every different element you need to preserve in mind so that you can technique people and establish associates successfully. This can also additionally furthermore help you with a variety of things. For one, it may assist making a decision which of the individuals inside the room are up for an interplay and which need to be left by myself.

During a talk, being watchful will help you to provide comments which may be pertinent to the difficulty handy. It also allow you to deliver suitable compliments so you ought to make the man or woman you're speaking to feel good about themselves. Practice being observant. Notice devices you may bring up in a communicate. Notice matters about the individual you're speakme to. This is a genuinely effective weapon when it comes to growing pals.

Smile!

A grin can and will flow an extended manner. If you're trying to method someone, do it with a smile. No one likes to be approached by the use of manner of someone who appears grumpy. If you need to make friends, do it with a grin too! It will improve the surroundings and the man or woman you're drawing near will in reality look in advance to speaking with you. Never underestimate what a pleasant grin may additionally moreover convey. A lot of friendships have in reality started with a unmarried grin. This might be actual for you as well. Just bear in mind, the subsequent time you approach a person, method them smiling.

Allow them to talk as nicely

While it's miles exquisite for you to speak about your self just so the alternative character might also moreover get to comprehend you higher, just undergo in thoughts that an wonderful way to create friends thru chats, the interplay itself desires to be a -way street. The one-of-a-type character needs to be talking as an awful lot as you do. The greater you open up about your self, the more they must as properly.

With this in mind, there are matters you could do to urge the alternative character to speak out greater inside the occasion that they're being extra quiet than you need them to be. The first and the outstanding approach to reap it's far to ask them questions. Keep asking them open-ended questions about the way to solution thoroughly. Whenever they do begin speakme, a exceptional trouble you can do to inspire them to preserve going is to reveal them you're definitely taking note of them. Listen to their every phrase. Lean in nearer to suggest motive. Nod your head every every now and then. These are diffused, tiny matters however they'll truely encourage and beautify the opportunity character.

Be attentive of your body language

As said earlier, you can suggest the alternative person that you are listening by using manner of moving your body in severa approaches. Aside from that, there are various unique topics that you may do to illustrate properly body language. Doing so will make you seem and experience extra snug. The character you're engaging with will likewise increase to feel snug with you as you move alongside.

For instance, you ought to keep away from crossing your fingers all of the time at the same time as chatting to someone. If your palms and arms revel in bizarre, certainly positioned them in your pocket. You need to keep away from slouching because it suggests exhaustion and soreness. Think on self notion and act assured. Your body language could possibly convey extra than your words ever may additionally want to. Make sure you're aware about it.

Maybe keep away from coming close to businesses at to begin with

You can be tempted to method a collection of people even as you're but studying this complete way. After all, if you can accomplish so well, you then genuinely'll continually have some of pals that rapidly. However, if contacting people is some thing you're no longer aware of doing however, I recommend you hold away of doing this for now.

Approaching a collection is a one-of-a-kind diploma of being socially in a position as compared to merely drawing close a unmarried individual. For now, pay hobby your hobby on one individual at a time. That way, you're more green and the interactions you'll have are extra non-public and crucial. Once you genuinely get the cling of drawing close to people and befriending them, you could next attempt to method a collection of buddies. For now, but, don't worry approximately this large chore honestly yet.

Set obstacles

There are limits in social interactions that should constantly keep in thoughts and respect. You may additionally take a look at this honestly or metaphorically. Literally talking, there need to constantly be a first rate hollow amongst you and the opposite man or woman. Breaking the touch barrier an excessive amount of is a threshold you need to in no manner cross. This is going for the talks you'll have with them as well. You may also ask inquiries approximately their lives, however you need to always don't forget to end up aware about their obstacles so that you can in no way cross that. If there's a query they pick no longer answering, then don't press your exact fortune.

You furthermore shouldn't ask inquiries which might be too personal if it's your first time speakme to that man or woman. At the equal time, you moreover mght ought to disclose facts about your self which might be too non-public. Find the border and be careful to no longer bypass beyond it.

Don't hesitate to provide advocate, if it's sought

Offering recommend is something pretty a few socially professional humans do. This permits unique dad and mom sense cushty with them, and it even makes them grow to be greater handy. However, at the same time as they do offer hints sometimes, they'll in no manner hand out unsolicited ones.

If you want to nicely approach human beings to installation buddies, this is something you moreover may moreover need to do. When you're speaking with someone and that they appear like they want counsel, do not be hesitant to provide one. However, if you can't provide any, make sure to moreover now not spout ridiculous or simply awful bits of propose. Just supply them out when you have some thing to say is probably beneficial. Also, you need to in no way hand them out if the alternative individual doesn't need it. Sometimes, a person really desires to vent and that they simply want you to pay interest. This is suitable too. Just offer an ear whilst presenting advocate isn't required.

Be empathetic

To be empathetic is to recognize and feel exactly what the opposite individual is feeling. It is a social and emotional tool you may use to gauge every one of a kind individual's thoughts and feelings so you can react consequently. Not best is this useful on the same time as speakme to a person, however it is also in the end one of the extraordinary things you could do to befriend every other person.

Empathy is particularly critical. That said, you need to spend no time within the use of it each time you're out and approximately and coming near humans. This may additionally moreover even make all of your encounters extra powerful and large for you. If you could empathize with absolutely everyone you meet, you'll spend your days drawing inside the feelings and mind of different parents. This is an in reality adorable problem to revel in.

This is how you may create friends. Approach absolutely everyone and be empathetic with them. Put your self in their shoes once they're speaking approximately their evaluations, each the coolest and the awful. You'll be able to connect to them better that way.

Be at a place you're comfortable in

One modest however useful factor you may additionally do is to go to places you're familiar in. If you're in a placing that's snug for you, you'll be able to method people and establish pals a long manner extra and not using a hassle. Whereas if you're in a scenario you discover discomforting, you'll surely spend most of some time trying to acclimate to the surroundings as a substitute of actually taking note of the individual you're going to be speaking to. With this in mind, prefer to high-quality mingle in settings in which you're cushty. Places you've already been to earlier than or new places with atmospheres which might be to your liking. This will make your enjoy plenty much less tough and masses greater splendid.

Approach People and Make Friends with the useful resource of Improving Your Social Skills

If you in reality want to technique human beings and make buddies correctly, aside from the use of what you've simply have a look at right here, you'll additionally need to dramatically increase your social capabilities as a whole. You'll want to turn out to be the socially adept character you need to be. That way, you'll be capable of make relationships effectively and gain the friends you want to have, regardless of in which you journey.

There are a number of of factors that play into enhancing your social capabilities. Thankfully, you'll have a ton of have a have a look at resources to resort to at the same time as perusing this web website. Read the articles proper here to build up considered one of a type social abilities which embody being available, studying the art of discussions, and dealing with severa social fears. The path beforehand of you is prolonged and complete with obstacles. But it will likely be as an alternative really worth it. For now, studies and exercise. Wherever you move, try to method humans and shape buddies. You may moreover sincerely be able to manufacture a couple of them.

Chapter 4: How To Initiate First Speak

Some humans seem to be born with the capability to begin up a communique, while others warfare to initiate casual talks. A critical social ability is knowing a manner to begin a verbal exchange. Knowing a way to start a communique may additionally additionally assist you enjoy greater relaxed and confident in severa social eventualities, whether or no longer or not you're trying to electrify a capability customer, strike up a communicate with a love interest, or sincerely speak with a present day acquaintance. Going to a celebration or probable a company feature may be uncomfortable if being in a massive organization is your best dread. Whether you're reclusive, shy, or excessively frightened, those varieties of social instances may be tremendously difficult.

Preparing beforehand of time is a very widespread method to lower scenario. Go over what you want to mention on your mind, examine with a coworker if feasible. Being properly-prepared is step one toward turning into a brilliant conversationalist.

If you're hesitant about organising a communication, strive this sort of three simple techniques first:

Maintain an positive thoughts-set: Stop being afraid of growing a mistake and consider on your abilties. Being excessively concerned approximately what you'll say subsequent ought to lead you to forget about approximately what you deliberate to say at the same time as speakme. Rather, purpose to preserve your recognition on what the opportunity side is pronouncing.

Take numerous deep breaths: You're more prone to be uptight in case you're tight and involved. Maintain a relaxed tone and permit the talk to float freely.

Introduce your self: One of the handiest techniques to get started is to actually introduce your self after which permit the alternative character do likewise. After this primary introduction, try and ask a simple query or make a clean remark to stimulate extra speak.

Tips on How to Start a Conversation

1. Keep It Pleasant: Your talk need to begin in a splendid tone. Avoid venting your emotions or voicing unsightly feedback. You can usually discover a few component correct to say, regardless matter how terrible things are.

Remark topics much like the weather, the food, the people you're with, or the occasion virtually. It's a fantastic technique to begin a subject by way of the usage of way of maintaining some component simple like I'm having a lovable time" and expect that the individual you choice to speak with is having a exceptional time as well. Even if the scenario isn't ideal, try to find out the coolest thing of things. A favorable statement is much more likely to generate a high first-rate reaction than a horrible one. It suggests that you are a pleasant character who's privy to what is going on. Keeping a satisfied thoughts-set additionally lets in humans loosen up. People might be greater inquisitive about having a talk with you as a reward.

2. Start Simple: A deep, philosophic, earth-shattering statement isn't critical to begin each outstanding dialogue. Simple preliminary phrases or enquiries are a incredible way to get the talk began. It may sound cliché to make compliments about the climate, the locale, or the meals, but there's a purpose why this style of advent works so efficaciously. It's a vital, simple technique to start a communicate with the aid of giving a few basis issue amongst human beings. Talking approximately minor stuff also can bring about deeper talks approximately person thoughts, backgrounds, pursuits, and particular

concerns that could help human beings construct social bonds.

3. Ask for Help: A better technique to start a debate is to ask a question. This gives you a purpose to have interaction with the opportunity individual further to letting them aid you. While employing this method, begin with a few element clear-cut that may be achieved with little strive. For example, you could query about the begin time of a seminar or routes to a given vicinity. Asking a fundamental enquiry can also need to bring about a similarly debate approximately certainly one of a kind topics, this is one of the benefits of this technique. Even after you've posed your question and the possibility individual has promised to help, you and your communique associate have made a type of mutual alliance. It's now as plenty as you to expose your appreciation and recognize yourself thinking about that they've provided their help. This

is a amazing time for every of you to get to comprehend each excellent better

4. Body Language: What we don't speak is regularly sincerely as remarkable as what you do. It's crucial to be privy to your nonverbal cues whilst starting a easy situation depend. Interest and exuberance may be showed with the useful resource of body language. A fine smile, a snug mind-set, and establishing eye contact, for one, may need to advocate that you definitely need to have a look at more about this distinct man or woman. Slouching, looking away, and frowning may also additionally deliver the advent that you are aggravated or disinterested inside the talk.

5. Listen and Expressing Interest: Trying to communicate with a person with whom you don't seem to have loads in commonplace may be daunting. Engaging the alternative individual to speak about their hobbies, artwork, or abilities is a clever approach to begin a talk in such contexts. Ask inquiries

like what the opportunity man or woman loves doing, then take note of what they respond. Everyone loves discussing their pastimes, therefore demonstrating a actual interest in what different human beings price can be a awesome communication starter.

6. Strike A Balance: There isn't always any one-length-fits-all" approach to having an notable communicate. The best conversations combo asking questions, taking note of what others have to say, and sharing private statistics. Asking open-ended questions that can't be responded with a easy positive" or no" also can be powerful. Instead of asking, Did you enjoy the speaker?" you can enquire, How did you like the speaker?" Learning the way to begin a communique is a critical expertise that might assist you construct social ties mainly settings. It may be problematic on the begin, mainly if you be stricken by shyness or social tension, however the exercising is

the important thing to turning into more comfortable speakme with human beings. Consider those trades to be a trial run. Your communication skills will boom as you begin interactions with human beings extra frequently.

7. Avoid Conversation Killers: Although it typically isn't emphasized sufficient, there are various subjects you need to keep away from addressing till you are distinctly cushty with the people you are speakme to. While your family can also release talks with opinion articles, gossip, reviews, and beside the point jokes in some unspecified time in the future of reunions, this is often now not a exceptional communication starter. There are other proper moments for sharing your perspectives or maybe trying to persuade someone but be confident such troubles are best in advance than attractive into a heated communique.

When it entails taking off a verbal exchange with a stranger, it's miles advocated to conform with the secure approach. This communication opener is much less daunting, but it notwithstanding the reality that disturbing conditions the other man or woman to react in some manner.

8. Be Funny: This doesn't recommend you want to carry out a stand-up act; crack some jokes and inform them a first rate yarn to get the talk began. You'll be stunned at how sharing exciting anecdotes may also furthermore inspire others to show their sentiments. Everyone likes guffawing, and laughing makes others experience relaxed. This is a extremely good approach to loosen up the ones tense parents and get them speakme. To trap the person's hobby, employ your wit. Demonstrate which you're a brief philosopher who appreciates wordplay, humorous jokes, and large chat. Use it if you have a extraordinary fun narrative, as lengthy because it's no longer too prolonged. If you deliver a lengthy tale that you haven't finished before, it could

now not earn you the reaction you anticipated

Chapter 5: Handle Uncomfortable Pauses Like An Professional.

As difficult as it could be to admit, the bulk of human beings spend a large amount of time idly analyzing thru social media, swiping on dating apps, or maybe gambling cell games. In specific phrases: This technology loves their telephones. In truth, a country wide 2021 ballot executed thru records.Ai indicated that most human beings spend a median of four.Eight hours an afternoon on their cellular devices — that's one-third of the hours they spend extensive wide awake, to place that into mind-set. Especially in this put up-lockdown generation, this immoderate time spent on video display units is probably considered to have positioned a chunk of a damper on one's social capabilities. Raise your hand if you've puzzled to yourself How do I humans?" at least as fast as considering that 2020? Yep — that is why it allows to understand the way to preserve a dialogue going.

Psychologist and inventor of Mental Drive Joshua Klapow, Ph.D. Thinks that the previous severa years have in reality produced demanding conditions with humans's functionality to connect to an extra IRL. We have had to alter to a loss of conversation and as a end result, our in-individual verbal exchange abilties have on not unusual been impacted," he says Bustle, regarding the suitable abilities to observe emotions and body language in addition to to live targeted for prolonged durations of time. We're rusty," affords Klapow. Sound familiar? Indeed.

Whether you're on a date, at the place of job, or speakme with a friend, you may find your self having a tough time dealing with a lull or uncomfortable silence. To help, proper here are some expert guidelines for a way to hold a communicate going.

1. Ask Open-Ended Questions

One of the simplest methods to preserve the talk going? Ask open-ended queries, suggests Klapow. If you're due to the fact the individual you're speakme to isn't imparting you with the same engagement or enthusiasm lower back, offer you with a question that takes extra than a certain or no response. They might not be collaborating because of the truth they're afraid or don't enjoy associated with the communicate, so strive asking questions you recognize they'll have a solution for. You may also moreover ask them significant questions about what they revel in, what their existence is like, and lots of others.," Klapow recommends.

2. Ask Them to Elaborate

Another trick? Make the possibility man or woman enjoy snug thru pushing them to percentage extra. Klapow believes it's OK to probe a touch to inspire them to open up. Asking a person to expound on what they will let you recognize is a strong approach to steer a far much less talkative character to show extra in their perspectives.

3. Talk about Topics That Interest Them

How to preserve a communique flowing and prevent an embarrassing lull.

If a discussion enters a halt, bear in mind the challenge subjects they appeared to be reacting to greater and pass there, recommends Klapow. Ask questions that allow the man or woman to talk approximately what's most snug to them," he tells Bustle. Or, if you're pals on social media, attempt to recall a few issue that jumped out in really one among their extra modern-day postings — whether or not or not it's a restaurant, a drink, or a fantastic dress, bringing it up will make certain to hobby them.

4. Ask About Their Likes & Dislikes

When the whole thing else fails or if you aren't that related with the individual you're speaking with, right away out inquire about gadgets they revel in and hate. Klapow notes this will get youngsters to speak. Pro tip: Try to stability the contributions with responses from you and inquiries from you to them," he suggests.

5. Mirror the Person You're Speaking With

One useful approach to reveal someone that you're there and engaged is to be conscious of your answers to what they percentage, certified social paintings accomplice Lexi Alberts says. To the degree that is permissible and cushty, echo others' vocabulary once they communicate about themselves," she tells Bustle. That will assist prevent setting words inside the other character's mouth, and may work an extended way towards a person feeling seen and heard via you." This can also involve refraining from making assumptions about what they're saying, and as an opportunity getting indicators from them and reacting with affirmation virtually in order that they apprehend you listen them.

6. Get Comfortable Being Authentic

For most individuals, close friends offer a secure location almost about social engagement. Depending on how close to you are to them, there need to be tiny safety systems. Be human," Klapow recommends. Point out the uncomfortable instances, phrase how you feel having the talks, and most significantly commentary on — if it's right — how adorable it's far to sincerely be with them." Showing that you're feeling snug enough to admit at the identical time as subjects become uncomfortable — even through a honest shaggy dog story — should make your buddy revel in sturdy and cushty as well, which also can assemble the keep in mind to your friendship.

No rely what venue your dialogue is accomplished in, Klapow urges you to concentrate on being your most honest self. Acknowledge that you're human, that lulls or faux pas would possibly possibly appear, and which you're sensible about connecting with the individual you're speakme to. After all, human connection is once more. It is probably scary to start talking to someone new. Never fear turning into friends with them. A easy Hello" is simple sufficient to initiate preliminary contact. But then you definately need to apprehend the manner to preserve a communicate going.

To help you boom the ones important relationships, right proper right here's the manner to keep a communication like a seasoned.

What Constitutes a Good verbal exchange?

A top notch dialogue is product of numerous additives. Here are some of the ones abilties which can also moreover maintain those uncomfortable silences at bay.

1. Active listening

Active listening is a fashion of hearing in which the emphasis is on really paying interest whilst the alternative person is speakme. Sometimes people pay attention to reply in place of being attentive to what their communique associate is saying. This key listening capability enables your discussion associate recognize that you are paying attention. It is a sign of emotional intelligence. Plus, you're much more likely to keep in thoughts greater of the chat later. You may also boom your lively listening through manner of repeating what you've got definitely heard decrease returned to the speaker. And by way of way of pronouncing lots tons less and listening extra.

2. Asking and answering questions

Another approach of demonstrating that you are a terrific listener is to ask questions.

Follow-up questions applicable to what the other individual stated may also deepen the discourse. Or you can question them approximately whatever you didn't quite maintain near or are interested by understanding more approximately. Again, this tells the man or woman you are talking to that you are simply interested in what they've got to say.

3. Finding mutual pursuits and similarities

While having a dialogue, keep your ears open for reports that you percentage in commonplace. Mutual interests may want to possibly provide you a few component to talk about and can preserve the dialogue going effortlessly. Finding commonalities can also assist boom not unusual ground and permit for a more first-class interplay. This is a critical component in a manner to maintain a speak moving without problems.

4. Having a motive for the discussion

Whether you've bumped into a colleague at the shop in any other case you're having a talk at a networking occasion, it's miles commonly excellent to have a reason in thoughts for the stumble upon. Having a described purpose guarantees the talk has course and isn't unsightly or awkward. If you discover that the discussion is stagnating, you may in all likelihood leverage the purpose of the verbal exchange to provide a present day-day communique subject.

How can the art of communication gain you within the administrative center?

Striking up a decent dialogue together with your coworkers extends past making corporation connections. Here's why mastering the art work of conversation is so powerful within the workplace.

1. Conversations generate our very private power

The artwork of verbal exchange provides to severa varieties of energy within the workplace. Specifically, it allows you establish referent strength thru manner of creating don't forget and recognize together with your coworkers, being a superb conversationalist may additionally even resource your effect over individuals you communicate with. Successful communication is a top notch contributor to powerful and inclusive management. Good conversation capabilities can assist to keep crew desires and techniques efficiently. This will installation higher do not forget with the parents that you are talking with. If a way to conduct a difficult communicate effectively, this can solidify your reputation as a in a function chief.

2. Networking boosts professional boom

Good conversation competencies raise your networking. In turn, this may beautify your social capital and encourage your professional development, no matter the truth that our credentials receives us inside the door, it's miles our ability to speak and make a extremely good have an impact on that promotes our careers.

three. Good paintings connections enhance employee happiness

Being able to preserve a verbal exchange is essential to creating and preserving terrific expert connections. In turn, powerful work connections sell a sense of belonging and growth worker morale.

4. Quality discussions increase performance and productivity

Healthy conversation amongst coworkers provides to ideal artwork relationships and worker happiness. These may enhance typical performance and manufacturing. You have to come to be better organized to teach and enlarge your coworkers too. With solid talking abilties, on-the-activity schooling will possibly be higher understood and take a bargain less time. This, in turn, want to contribute to higher performance and manufacturing as properly.

How to Keep a Conversation Going and Never Run Out of Things to Say

One of the number one annoying conditions you could experience at the identical time as looking for to make new pals is the uncomfortable silence. Encountering this situation is so ugly that it might even motive you to keep away from meeting new humans in the first place, but there may be a manner to get past it.

In the past, I fought with this so much that I felt it may never be addressed. I even assumed it needed to do with my DNA or something... however I proved myself wrong as soon as I learnt the way to restore it. Not expertise a manner to keep a communication going can harm your social existence, however in case you apprehend the manner to preserve those terms flowing, you can meet, speak to, and get to understand quite a bargain genuinely everybody you like—developing excellent opportunities for friendship, a laugh and shared sports activities which you could otherwise have not noted out on. Another trouble isn't always getting to know to get within the mood for talking. If you spend a entire day operating or studying analytical or logical matters, and also you don't realize a way to transition from that, then it would take pretty some time to warmth up and begin engaging with others socially. You might also moreover moreover conquer this without a doubt with the useful resource of way of obtaining a few new skills, together with the ones stated beneath. Once you do this, you'll have the capability to talk to new humans, and make pals, masses extra resultseasily.

Let's get you began with a handful of clean, however robust techniques on a manner to be a remarkable conversationalist:

No Filtering

This is the reflex that allows you to mention anything is going on for your mind. No filtering, no checking with oneself can also I sound cool if I stated this?" None of that. The best method to exercise that is to begin doing it with human beings you shape of understand—do you dare to do it? It's exciting to apprehend that you're entitled to talk some thing is on your mind, and no individual goes to criticize you for it. As lengthy as you don't say some aspect which could put you in prison, you're okay! People don't care an excessive amount of approximately how notable" what you're pronouncing is, because they're too concerned on how THEY are discovering. Get it? If so, allow's pass on...

Interesting, inform me more!"

This works 99% of the time. It's a dependable technique, and it really works in particular properly for novices. People want to apprehend which you're interested by what they have got to say, so if you show a few hobby, they'll linger round and want to talk to you even greater.

All of the oh! That's thrilling...", Hmm, I've never heard of that", Hmm, cool!" These are responsive quantities of speech that screen to the possibility person that you're in fact listening, and that's fairly tremendous to them.

Stories from anywhere

Everyone is acquainted with that tales juice-up talks, but most individuals in reality communicate approximately reminiscences from very non-public existence. You don't should draw in your personal revel in even as speaking to someone: you could make use of reminiscences from everywhere, from stories that befell to human beings you realise, to the ones you got right here for the duration of thru the radio, TV, magazines, and so forth.

How are you able to comprise the tales into your communication? The trick is to first understand that you can make use of them. You've already heard them, and the more captivating or weird they may be, the tougher they may be to neglect about, so that you're all ok. Your mind doesn't lose them. When a person discusses some thing associated with any of these, sincerely percent the story, although it's not out of your life. It can be any loopy anecdote, quick or extended, beautiful, or genuinely awkward—really use it!

Someone adore chatting to folks that can sincerely communicate some thing actually like that. These techniques want to get you commenced out, however if you need to take it to a complicated diploma—to the component wherein you may without a doubt have amusing at the equal time as speakme to all of us, meet the proper people you need on your life, and be capable of make friends with them speedy—then I endorse which you take a hint time to research extra approximately how conversations paintings. If you try this, you'll make conversations a ways more thrilling, with herbal ease, preserving off all awkward silences that would prevent you from assembly the proper pals which you would like to have round.

The Bottom Line

Now which you recognize the techniques to preserve a verbal exchange persevering with, the subsequent component you need to do is hire this form of techniques the subsequent time you chat with a person.

Don't overload yourself attempting to appoint these type of methods at the equal time, get acclimated to 1 in every of them first. When you can master one of the techniques, you'll experience extra solid to use the alternative strategies in your next talks too!

You revel in it...The loss of life of your communicate.

"Some get the crash cart!!!"

You're standing there, it looks as if hours given which you've were given talked. The ice for your drink slowly melts.

We've all been there, thinking the way to keep a communication going at the equal time as:

Making small conversation with a co-worker before the Zoom meeting starts.

Meeting a trendy man or woman at a outdoor BBQ.

Sitting subsequent to an acquaintance at some stage in happy hour.

When we're capable of maintain that speak persevering with, we will amplify new friends, higher employment opportunities, and become greater a achievement.

So how can we do it?

Here are five "Dig Questions" to steal:

"Tell me more approximately x."

"Why x?"

"What become that second like for you?"

"When did you first apprehend x?"

"Knowing what now, ought to you have even though carried out x?"

With the ones questions, we're graduating to deeper conversational ranges. We're asking questions geared to permit us apprehend more about who that character is, and what it's far need to be them. With Spokes and the Talk Show Host Mindset, you are putting the conversational spotlight on the other individual.

People adore that.

People apprehend studying they have a few element in not unusual with humans, when they do, it signals that they belong to the same tribe. Sometimes, the links are smooth (equal enterprise, equal alma college or similar conference) (identical business enterprise, same alma mater or equal conference). Sometimes, they're teased out through discussion, on the identical time as you realize that you every are into the equal difficult to understand band, watch their face light up as you tell them.

Action step: When the "Same right right here!" crop up, do no longer permit them to skip like ships in the night time time. Call them out! The extra shared connections you have were given were given with someone, the much more likely you'll take to each other.

Finally, realise that pauses WILL show up. They take region in every talk, they best emerge as uncomfortable pauses in case you conceive of them as being "awkward". Sometimes, pauses is probably vital.

After I ask a query on my, there can be a completely palpable urge to fill the "vacuum" of stillness that arises after asking a query. It's appropriate to allow the opposite character a second to growth a response, frequently this results in a higher discussion due to the fact that I gave them the room to bear in mind. If there is a conversational pause, and also you'd need to transport out of it, keep in thoughts the use of the subsequent script:

"Oh, I genuinely recalled this..."

You can also use this to segue to some different trouble depend out of your tale vault, or you could say "Tell me greater about x." in that you deliver up some factor they've got spoken approximately, this sort of interest, adventure or profession. The primary difficulty we want to keep away from at the same time as gaps come is the internal monologue of "Oh my, this is some other embarrassing pause, what need to I talk about?!"

Chapter 6: Conversation Gone Awry (What To Say)

Well it did now not move properly.

You're sad, he's dissatisfied and you are in all likelihood wondering what to do now, earlier than we turn out to be back wherein we commenced, permit's take a breath, halt and regroup.

First off, ensure you deal with your self. Do you want to get help from a pal or communicate with a professional who can assist collectively along with your unique scenario? If sure, skip to the phase in which you could discover a choice of alternatives you can gain out to for help. If you are OK, allow's take a look at techniques to refocus and pay interest so that you can face the problem reachable and perhaps no longer wind yourself returned right here again. Feel such as you arrived in the midst of some element?

You've arrived in an ABC Everyday 'select out your very very very own adventure' that exposes the right results of the gender hollow for girls in heterosexual relationships. And searching at what we're able to do approximately it, you can certainly have a look at the tale, or you can take some recommendation and attempt it out in actual life. It's as lots as you.

Take me to the start of the adventure please!

Plan to try over again later

When a talk is going poorly, it is generally due of misconceptions which depart each events feeling angry and omitted. If you could pinpoint wherein subjects went incorrect and why, it could help with a modern-day technique subsequent time, but a horrible reaction within the speak is not a fail. Stopping an problem if it's far going nowhere is a clever idea – you may try all over again later. If you do not face your troubles, you may not repair them.

Tips to Prepare for a Discussion

Make a time to have a speak about what is troubling you. Stick on your set time for that communicate.

"Gather your proof" – think about what it's miles you need to mention and what elements you need the other character to recognize. If you choice to break up the house duties extra equitably, retaining a report of who does what might also assist you show your argument or discover in which the problems sincerely are.

Write down dot elements of what you choice to unique. It would in all likelihood help you make a decision what you need to speak about.

If you recognise you normally generally tend to become labored up or agitated, try slowing your respiratory to assist maintain you calm. Breathe via your nose to maintain your respiration slower.

Elements of a splendid talk

Here are a few fundamental hints for making each talk a higher one:

Express your sentiments the use of "I" sentences, like: "I experience taken as a proper as quickly as I make supper every unmarried night."

Ask open inquiries. Questions like: "What are your views surrounding that?" or "What's the worst component about it for you?"

Listen to what the opportunity character says and mirror once more to them what you apprehend they may be saying. If you've got misunderstood, allow them to clarify their argument another time and try no longer to be dismissive or protecting. Face each extraordinary and do no longer allow yourself get sidetracked through way of other topics. Eye touch and bodily contact may also help you live centered on each specific.

Show empathy. You may not agree when they declare they cook every unmarried night time, however you could sympathize with how they may be feeling. "I can understand why you'll revel in that manner" or "I can see that this makes you quite sad".

You do not must try this alone. How to accumulate help if you need it

Sometimes you in reality want a third person to help you've had been given an splendid speak, it's miles not the cease of a dating to acquire beneficial resource

Summary. We are at least 75% answerable for how others regard us. Our vocal and nonverbal symptoms indicate to others the amount of...Greater

Every character is at the least 75% liable for how others regard them. Our vocal and nonverbal acts limit or beautify the opportunities of others. For example, if someone asks, How are you?" as he or she passes via, you understand higher than to expose spherical and walk with them which will deliver an extended response. By continuing to walk by the use of way of, the person conveys that simply a nod or short assertion is predicted. However, if that individual had been to pause and appearance you in the eye even as asking the identical query, your options trade. Their actions has endorsed more than a reflexive response.

We're all creatures of dependancy, and conversation styles assist us keep away from having to consider the whole lot we communicate. But at the same time as we lapse into styles amazing due to the fact we've did now not installation opportunity response options, we emerge as predictable. If you are famend for a predisposition to keep away from conflict of words, for example, humans may additionally moreover produce conditions on the way to strain you to shy away, express regret, or walk away. You relinquish a piece of your seventy five% obligation. That's not proper! But if we have had been given a repertory of responses and comebacks at our fingertips, we may also pick out of recurring styles. For instance, it's viable to learn how to regard certain nasty inquiries as purpose inquiry, find out some detail of commonplace experience in an apparently ludicrous statement, or respond to an insult as although it had been inadvertent. In this manner, as an alternative of having victimized thru the usage of repeated styles, we grow to be arbiters of what occurs to us. Such competence is specifically vital in adverse political situations because of the reality what's said is often not what's intended. Highly politicized artwork areas call for a diploma of street smarts to live on and prevail. It's critical to apprehend effective techniques of reacting to traumatic activities.

What if a person tells you one difficulty, but you then pay interest that she or he said some thing very certainly one of a type to others? This isn't unusual in tremendously political institutions. Should you permit it pass? Hold a grudge? Never accept as true with that individual over again? Address the matter without delay? With a repertory of replies, you have have been given options. You might also also be able to avoid comparable conditions from happening to you inside the destiny through deciding on an powerful reaction at once after the correct offense – a reaction that activates the offending person to assume two times subsequent time. Whether you're new to broadening your reply repertoire or a pro hand, it's important to have more than one replies efficiently available. The following R-List" of labeled strategies might also help you purchased precisely that. When reacting to a probable horrible state of affairs, facility with them also can moreover assist thrust back harm to an crucial connection or neutralize a risk on your credibility:

Reframe — Cast the situation in a modern-day mild. Describe the opposite man or woman's remarks or conduct in a manner that behooves destiny exchanges. If a person says, I don't want to combat over this," a useful reframing of that declaration is, This is a speak, honestly not a struggle. And you're a first-rate debater, as I recollect."

Rephrase — Say the terms in a new, a first-rate deal plenty much less terrible way. Should someone accuse you of getting lengthy beyond on too aggressively at a meeting, you may say, I come to be passionate." If you're regarded as obstinate, you may solution, I'm pretty determined even as a few element is essential to a a fulfillment strive." Rather to permit misguided or insulting language through, provide substitutes.

Revisit – Use a previous achievement to reinterpret a present failure. If the women and men taking component in a communicate have a preceding records of green interactions, it would assist to remind them of beyond success and their functionality to set up not unusual floor: We have a strong tune record working together. No reason to adjust that now."

Restate – Clarify or divert poor phraseology. Anyone may moreover unwittingly offer offense or initiate war. At such situations, it's useful to use one in every of my favored strategies: Give them an opportunity to do the right thing. Surely there's some other way to word that" or Did you suggest what I don't forget I heard?" are exceptional strategies to influence a person to check and modify what become stated.

Request — ask an inquiry. When in query approximately a person's meaning, one logical method is to confirm your impressions through interrogating them earlier than responding negatively: Would you give an explanation for for me what you supposed virtually then?"

Rebalance — regulate the opposite character's power. People relinquish electricity needlessly after they permit every different man or woman to reason them to unsightly or undermine their manner. Often, such strength imbalance can be modified. One approach is to restrict the effect on you along side your thoughts-set — refusing to get outraged — or through placing forward, Fortunately, I'm no longer with out problem angry, especially with the aid of 1-off activities like this."

Reorganize — Change the significance of the concerns. Direct the controversy far from private issues by means of using emphasizing on approach. For instance, one answer may be, We seem to agree at the what but are having some troubles with the how." In this method, you lessen the issue in half of of. The emphasis is now on without a doubt one component of what could in any other case appear to be an insurmountable impasse.

Versatility differentiates wonderful communicators from those who are pushed and dragged thru talks — and lifestyles. The subsequent time you meet what appears to be a hurdle, whether or now not because of offense or perplexity, take a look at the sorts of comebacks above. Experimentation is the pleasant way to become at least 75% answerable for how we're treated. Otherwise, we spend most of our days trapped in ruts, being predictable, and engaging in nowhere. There's no pleasure or reward in that.

So often, our motive is misconstrued or messages are misunderstood as a result of lousy speech and verbal exchange skills.

Prevent this from occuring thru way of performing the following:

1. Use the technology at your disposal

Make benefit of your technical alternatives. Change the backdrop of your emails or consist of emoji and gifs to your messages.

These will brighten up your on-line discussions and help you stand out from every person else who's the usage of the easy settings.

2. Ensure there are not any distractions

Just as you need to pay interest on the equal time as having a face-to-face dialogue, so need to you even as taking component in on line conversations.

Focus for your verbal exchange. Don't chat for your telephone and write at the identical time thinking about your preoccupation is probably seen to the receiver. When there are distractions surrounding you, you also are more prone to make errors in the communication.

By minimizing any distractions, you could guarantee that your conversations are correct and on path. Then you obtained't have to spend time afterwards clarifying up misconceptions and uncertainty.

three. Don't squander human beings's time

Make fine that there can be a proper purpose in your message. If the trouble or problem can be dealt with with a brief cellphone call, then do it that manner.

Knowing what to call about and what to e mail about may additionally additionally take some exercise. But the profits to the superb and efficacy of your expert relationships can be well well worth it.

four. Take notes

During highly essential actual-time on line discussions, taking notes ensures which you don't lose any key statistics ultimately.

Taking notes can even ensure that you gained't spend extra time with the aid of having to re-touch the mother and father engaged within the online assembly to gather records which have become brought.

5. Do an interest collectively on line

With a large amount humans working from home, we might also additionally often feel by myself and unconnected. We can assist reduce this with the aid of the use of collaborating in on-line sports activities.

Playing a web venture or taking a virtual tour with pals or art work colleagues can also help enhance your connections.

6. Don't be terrified of small chat

Small chat is a vital thing of in-individual encounters and must not be neglected whilst online.

If we certainly provide attention to industrial employer or the challenge on hand at the same time as on-line, we reduce the fine of our conversation via making it appear extra impersonal than it should be.

7. Know whilst to terminate the communicate

Knowing while and the way to complete a speak is another talent in the art of terrific verbal exchange. It applies to all talks that we have got, whether or not or no longer in-person or online. But stopping online chats can also additionally additionally frequently be a bit hard.

During a video discussion, try and interpret the alternative individual's body language. Try to choose up on non-verbal signs and symptoms that advocate it's time to location the dialogue to an end. For instance, they may be performing bored, or you may every be beginning to repeat yourselves.

Have numerous well mannered conversation closers handy and rehearse them absolutely so that they float results at the same time as the immediately is good.

Chapter 7: Questions That Make Small Chat Simpler.

7 Small Talk Topics for Starting Friendly Conversations

1. Introductions

Before you may get to apprehend someone, it's a fantastic concept to introduce yourself.

You can also introduce yourself to all and sundry you don't understand, or to remind a person you've met previously who may want to possibly have forgotten you. When you're introducing yourself, you may encompass a small piece of records like in that you first met, or what you do. You might also moreover use your English have a look at as a verbal exchange starter.

Examples:

Good morning! We continuously drink coffee at the equal time yet we've in no way talked in advance than. My call is [Your Name]."

Hello, how are you these days? My name is [Your Name]. I'm currently analyzing English so please allow me apprehend if I make any errors."

Hi Angela. You might not take into account me however we met at Tom's Christmas party ultimate 12 months. I'm [Your Name]."

2. Universal Topics

Topics which may be hooked up may be shared by way of nearly everyone.

Things just like the weather, cutting-edge-day records, sports and amusement are typically appropriate verbal exchange starters, particularly whilst you're speakme to a collection—even though one character doesn't without a doubt follow sports, someone else within the institution may additionally furthermore.

Although the ones subjects are spoken about thru many, some people won't be enthusiasts of sports activities activities activities, or may not follow leisure statistics, so if you could, try to match human beings's hobbies to the situation you chose. For example, if you've heard people discussing about essential records gadgets within the beyond, you could try to chat about a data tale from these days.

Examples:

Did you observe the Oscars very last week? I can't accept as true with Leonardo DiCaprio in the end received one!"

This climate is wild! It modified into chilly yesterday and nowadays I came in with an open jacket. I hope it remains warmness, don't you?"

That basketball interest the previous day had me hooked to my seat. Wasn't that a high-quality store on the very give up?"

3. The Day

If you're no longer positive what venture to speak about, or don't have a few issue fascinating to say, you could virtually ask a person approximately their day, or you may speak approximately yours.

For example, you can ask them:

How have become your day? / How has your day been to date?

How have you ever ever ever been feeling nowadays?

What have you ever been doing these days?

Has a few component incredible befell in recent times?

What are you planned for after artwork?

Are you performing some issue thrilling after paintings?

You also can alternate records approximately your day and the way you're doing, but attempt to keep a balance of speakme and listening, so that you every get to talk the identical quantity (and also you're not sincerely speaking approximately your self the whole time).

Even if the person looks like they've been having a horrible day, you may make it brighter in reality by way of the use of making small chat! Make cautious not to ask inquiries which is probably too non-public, and rather provide a few kind phrases of help.

Examples:

Hey there. You look like you're having a hard day. I hope subjects gets better for you."

Good morning! I went tenting on Saturday, and of path it poured all day. Was your weekend any higher?"

The day is sort of performed! Do you have got were given any thrilling plans for the night time?"

4. The Workplace

Some talks are best suitable in a expert surroundings.

Stay even a whole lot much less personal at art work than in extra informal locations, and keep away from gossiping (speakme about one-of-a-kind folks that aren't there)! Instead, you'll probable speak about the day, an upcoming birthday celebration or meeting, or inquire about the character's profession.

Examples:

Hi Tom. How are topics doing over on the IT branch these days?"

Good morning. I'm eagerly looking in advance to the birthday party after paintings nowadays. I pay attention Pam brought her excellent carrot cake!"

What a hectic day. This is the number one time I've gotten up from my seat all day! Are you busy too?"

5. Observations

Some of the greatest small communicate is prepared where you and your discussion companion are placed.

It's a few detail you each share, so there's no chance that they acquired't apprehend what you're speakme approximately. Look round and discover a few aspect to assertion about, or take a look at your accomplice and find out some thing great to congratulate them on. Nothing makes folks sense better than a honest praise!

Examples:

I adore your footwear in recent times, they absolutely supply your ensemble collectively."

Did you spot? They sooner or later repaired the moderate in the smash room. It's been broken for about a month!"

Hey Pam, your cookies final night time time time had been splendid! Thank you for developing those for the birthday celebration."

6. Common Interests

When you have a few aspect similar along with your speaking associate, it indicates you have had been given some detail to talk about. Find a mutual pal (a person you each recognise) or a shared hobby or interest, and you'll have some element to speak about.

Keep in thoughts that English people seldom actually pronounce the term hobby," so asking What are your hobbies?" sounds bizarre and unnatural. Try asking questions alternatively, based on observations.

Examples:

My cousin stated you final night time. I didn't understand you knew her! Where did you meet?"

I observed your hat had a Yankees emblem. Are you a lover of baseball too?"

I attempted making cookies like yours ultimate night time and that they have become out horrible. How do you're making them so right?"

7. Questions

You may have observed through now that most of these small chat examples have some element in common: They ask questions. A smart approach to begin a communicate is to make a declaration, then ask a question. This stops the talk from finishing for your reply (and making topics hundreds extra unpleasant!).

When asking questions, pay interest as loads as you talk, and don't skip too non-public collectively together with your queries. And keep in mind to maintain topics exquisite!

Examples:

Hey, I heard you have got been considering getting a present day domestic dog. Did you discover one?"

I've been trying to ask you this for some time: how lengthy have you ever been jogging right right right here?"

Your hair usually appears cute. What hair merchandise do you use?"

The next time you're repute with someone and no man or woman is chatting, you understand what to do!

Chapter 8: The Basics Of Good Conversation

While most people are comfortable making verbal exchange with pals and family, some human beings can with out problems flow into beyond this boundary and communicate to every person approximately some thing. If this type of interaction appears unfathomable to you, there are various topics that you could do to make speakme with genuinely everyone at any time, not fine possible however viable, and maybe, with workout, a few detail that is straightforward and amusing to do. While beginning a communique is protected in financial disaster five, you'll locate that you are more prepared to carry out that, if you spend some time considering the subsequent number one subjects every precise communication has in common first.

Make it clean you care about what the opportunity individual is pronouncing:

You might be surprised how masses much less complicated it's far to speak to an entire stranger in case you use the primary part of the communication to make it clear that you care approximately what the alternative person is pronouncing.

In famous, people are much more likely to open up and remember you interesting if you ask them masses of questions as this indicates you are interested by reading new subjects. This may also moreover make the alternative person greater comfortable and much more likely to share an excellent extra big communication. Always make certain to hold the amazing quantity of eye contact, as a minimum 50 percentage of the time even as speaking and as a minimum 70 percentage of the time on the identical time as listening further to listening actively as defined in financial disaster three.

Balance the conversation:

It is crucial to ensure than any communique you get into is one that has the right combination of backward and forward among you and the alternative man or woman. If you are shy with the aid of way of way of nature, then the extremely good way to get the proper glide is to invite some open ended questions which you think will deliver the opportunity man or woman plenty to speak approximately. After you have got were given asked them to difficult on their opinions a couple of times you have to feel greater snug approximately leaping in. Having a balanced communication is important because otherwise the opportunity character is probably going to experience as even though they will be being interrogated and begin to revel in uncomfortable, at worst; or, at extraordinary, definitely sooner or later lose interest and bypass on. Everyone likes speakme approximately themselves; most people don't experience doing so indefinitely.

If you discover your self in a scenario in which nerves purpose you to every speak too much or to freeze up and no longer communicate enough. In either state of affairs it's miles critical to take a second to breathe and recognition in advance than smiling in a way that proclaims you are slightly, however no longer appreciably, embarrassed through your actions earlier than redirecting the communique as appropriate, ideally with the useful resource of the use of choosing a ultra-modern verbal exchange subject matter related to the cause you and the opposite individual are every in the same area at the same time. If this takes place it's miles essential to not attention on it as soon as it has handed, people like notable individuals who famend their flaws without apologizing profusely for them. As lengthy as you downplay the awkward 2d you'll be notable.

Always have some difficulty to mention:

If you traditionally have a tough time growing with communique topics this might be due to the reality you aren't keeping up at the types of preferred subjects that human beings talk approximately. Know your audience and start retaining abreast of the topics which you comprehend they are interested by. If you are trying to be greater conversational in well-known, they preserve in mind preserving tabs on cutting-edge cultural dispositions, song or technological or clinical discoveries. Avoid speaking approximately politics besides you're confident you percent the same views because the alternative person.

Chapter 9: The Basics Of Bad Conversation

Once you've got a higher concept of what suitable communication consists of, the subsequent detail you'll need to do is avoid the subsequent communication killers if you need the opportunity individual to paste round prolonged sufficient to help you workout steps three-10.

Parroting:

If you and a few other person are having a communique, but in area of a from side to side interaction among people, all you are doing is repeating their evaluations whilst adding little else to the conversation, then unfortunately, it isn't in reality a communication. This is parroting and whilst some humans obtained't lose interest with this form of non-verbal exchange, they probable aren't those you really want to speak to except. Even if you percentage the equal evaluations as the person you're speakme with, it's far vital to continuously make an effort to characteristic something tremendous to the communique in case you need the opportunity individual to go again a long way from the communication with an opinion for your reviews.

Emotionless verbal exchange:

Regardless of the way thrilling your stories or mind-set on modern-day activities might be, in case you don't percentage them within the right manner then no man or woman may be able to keep their interest extended enough to pay attention the recollections or agree/disagree with your evaluations. Memorable conversation is alive with emotion and emphasis that travels amongst everyone worried in it. Bad conversation, rather can only ever limp alongside, prepared to be positioned out of its misery. In order to hold extra emotion, it may be beneficial to recollect your voice just like the song of a roller coaster. Instead of maintaining topics flat and boring, combination it up with vocal versions which might be appropriate for the conversation you are having. Don't forget about to emphasize with hand motions similarly to a manner to promote mainly emphatic moments.

Predictable communication:

If you're the form of individual who, inside the center of the communication, continuously excuses your self by means of manner of pronouncing exactly in which you are going, or constantly makes use of the space of a communique as actually a time for little greater than a literal transmission of records amongst parties then the humans you are speakme with may additionally additionally take into account you a predictable, and therefore uninteresting, conversationalist. If you experience as regardless of the reality that the conversations you are having are too literal, then you may find out achievement via being extra playful. Joke around, make off the wall feedback occasionally, attempt to aggregate matters up with a piece frivolity and you need to be aware super people becoming more engaged with what you're saying.

Narcissistic communique:

Even if what you're announcing is said in a manner this is exciting, if all you ever talk about is your self, then human beings can be clearly grew to end up off from speakme with you. Those who're unsure of the way to continue conversationally frequently fall into the lure of speaking approximately themselves, or no longer talking sufficient and every are further as lousy. Branch out in terms of verbal exchange subjects and only speak approximately your self if the tale has a humorous completing or is relevant to the current conversation.

Sentence hijacking:

While in a communication, if the other person is speakme and you finish their sentence for them then you definitely in reality definately have honestly come to be a communique hijacker. Except in specially acquainted situations or those which may be about coming to a mutual consensus, that is commonly taken into consideration disrespectful to the person who have become speakme. What's worse, in case you get it incorrect you then are being disrespectful similarly to indicating that what you said is more crucial than what the real conversation come to be about. This then motives the communique to grow to be disjointed and thrown off the glide in a way that can be hard to recover from.

Instead of assuming that you apprehend what the alternative character goes to say, offer you with a query to similarly decide their specifics before transferring beforehand. If you are in a habit of finishing unique people's sentences, the tremendous way to interrupt yourself of that addiction is through surely being aware of it as this need to possibly save you you from speakme in advance than you have were given the time to censor yourself. Don't beat yourself up if it doesn't correct the trouble , it's going to get simpler with workout.

Chapter 10: Learn To Listen

When you're in a conversation, it's miles sincerely as vital to make the alternative person experience as even though you are listening as it is to be actively engaged in whatever it's far they may be announcing. It is crucial to make the effort to pay attention with all your senses, and make it clean to the other man or woman which you without a doubt recognize some thing it's miles they may be speaking about. This is what's known as energetic listening and perfecting the strategies below will help make sure your frame is constantly on message.

Physical symptoms of listening

Smile:

Smiling at the proper instances at the same time as you're listening says that you recognize what the opportunity character is saying, or agree considerably with the difficulty being discussed or the precise facts being conveyed. When brought to a easy head nod, a grin is a way to mention which you apprehend what's being asked of you and you'll pass in advance and do it.

Eye contact:

Depending on how many human beings you're talking to and what else is going on throughout the communique, making eye contact is a awesome way for the alternative celebration to understand that you are being attentive to what they're announcing. Ensure you keep sufficient eye contact to reveal you've got got an hobby at the same time as now not preserving it so cautiously that it's far seen as inappropriate.

Posture:

The posture you operate at the same time as listening can say masses about your mind on the statistics inside the communication being conveyed. If you're actively listening, you may need to make it a element of leaning in the direction of the individual that is talking. You will need to characteristic to this through each resting your head in your hand on the identical time as looking the speaker or tilt your head to the aspect slightly to suggest you're listening.

Mirroring:

Mirroring the moves and mannerisms of the character you are listening to is a subconscious manner of permitting them to comprehend that you every are at the same net page. This need to look natural, but, as being found trying to mimic positive expressions will make it appear which you aren't listening the least bit. Alternatively, in case you begin mimicking the opposite person after which begin doing all your personal gestures or expressions and see them mimic you, you may understand you have got were given control of the conversation.

Don't appear distracted:

Even in case you are listening carefully, doing such things as looking at your smartphone, fidgeting, or nitpicking your appearance will all supply the speaker the concept of the alternative. Give the character you're listening to your complete hobby and they'll anticipate you are listening more nicely as a end result.

Remember key elements:

If you need to reveal the other individual that you have been genuinely listening, one of the amazing methods to achieve this is to preserve in thoughts key pieces of statistics approximately a verbal exchange you had previously. Don't worry about remembering the info, the gist of the conversation can be sufficient to purpose them to react favorably in your attempt.

Ask questions:

While many people who experience awkward in verbal exchange also can moreover agree with that asking questions is a notable manner to intend you weren't paying interest; in fact, it's far a super way to expose you fee what the possibility individual is pronouncing hundreds which you want to ensure you get it right. The questions you're asking must seem as even though they're digging deeper at the priority, now not in reality rehashing what has already been said.

Clarification:

Much like with asking questions, requesting clarification on what has been stated, assuming the information have not already been clarified is a top notch manner to make it clean to the other individual that you are sincerely invested in what they have got to say. It is crucial to invite for rationalization all of sudden, however, as breaking it up can reason the verbal exchange to experience stilted an unnatural.

Summarization:

At the give up of the communique, a extremely good way to make it clear you have been listening the entire time is to summarize the communique as stated to make sure which you and the speaker had been on the equal web page. Again, this indicates you will positioned the communication into movement, no longer which you weren't paying hobby.

Chapter 11: Dealing With Awkward Silences

No matter how properly any communique is going, there are normally going to be moments at the same time as all and sundry concerned runs out of things to mention at the equal time. This is flawlessly herbal, but, and can be effects conquer if you don't blow them out of percentage and alternatively attempt the severa pointers described underneath.

Consider why the silence passed off:

Depending on the character of the conversation which you are having, the reality that there can be a silence in the end of the communique might not even be awkward. If you and the alternative person are talking whilst additionally doing a little other project, then it would really be a function of the individual of the communication that result in the silence. Additionally, some humans might not even like small speak and as an possibility enjoy more snug inside the direction of a silence. Consider how the opportunity individual seems to be responding to the silence before assuming that it's miles automatically via some way your fault.

Don't overemphasize the silence:

Depending on the reason the silence came about, it's miles vital to no longer get so stressful about it that you perform a little factor that in the long run makes it worse in place of higher. There is continuously a risk that the opportunity person hasn't considered the silence awkward and calling attention to it's going to simplest make the scenario worse in vicinity of better. Instead of disturbing about it, located your thoughts to artwork bobbing up with a way to interrupt the silence.

Consider opportunity topics of communication:

If your communication has hit a lull, take a few moments to consider continuing the current train of idea in advance than as an opportunity thinking about in which to transport the verbal exchange next.

Start with the aid of the use of considering preceding communication threads which have been placed apart and note if you can ask a related question to get things moving all over again in the right course. If not anything jumps out at you proper away, then it'll in all likelihood be time to do not forget a modern difficulty rely of conversation. The splendid location to start is with a few issue associated with the cause you are both in the equal vicinity on the identical time or why you started speaking within the first location. Remember, if the silence is awkward, then it is possibly that the alternative birthday party can be thankful for a modern trouble matter variety of conversation so it is important to now not be afraid to throw one to be had.

Comment on it:

While it received't constantly be suitable to comment on the silence, it'll be the right desire sometimes. This is mostly a legitimate communication method if the verbal exchange died down because of a totally particular motive. You can downplay the silence if it is because the opportunity person didn't have some problem to mention to a query you asked, make a shaggy dog tale approximately the purpose for a silence, or perhaps touch upon it as a way to interrupt the anxiety. Whatever choice you go together with, it's miles essential which you have a cutting-edge direction to take the communication in afterwards if you don't want to turn out to be proper in which you began.

Know even as to be verbose:

Sometimes awkward silences stand up due to the fact the opposite man or woman has said some detail that they anticipated you to touch upon at length and you as an alternative replied with a one-phrase reaction. Keeping a verbal exchange going is a 2-man or woman hobby, and this now and again manner speaking at duration approximately something which you in any other case aren't all that eager to speak about. If you discover your self in this example, hold up the from side to side until you manage to find out a manner to transport the conversation to a more brilliant subject remember.

Utilize the silence:

If you have been planning on exiting a communique especially quickly except, there are few better instances to make your exit than while a silence obviously takes place. Sometimes silences stand up because of the reality there is no longer something left to mention and in case you don't take the exit at the same time as it's far supplied you and the opportunity man or woman will come to be stuck in a clumsy publish-communique communique in which not something exciting may be stated for a couple of minutes until the silence gadgets in yet again. Know whilst to get out on a excessive word and don't revel in overly-devoted to any communique, specifically with a stranger.

Chapter 12: Starting A Conversation

Now that you have discovered out what can turn a conversation from impartial to both suitable or horrible, it is time to start considering the quality way to begin a communique with a stranger no matter the time or the area. Before you get started it's far critical to apprehend that making communique is a talent because of this it's going to get less complicated with exercising, however additionally that it's going to best get a great deal less hard with exercising. While you are fine to make a few errors while you've got come to be the preserve of it, surely hold in thoughts that the subsequent time will continually be much less complex.

Start with a compliment:

One of the very super techniques to begin a communication with a stranger is thru complimenting them on both an difficulty in their look or a few trouble that they will be currently doing. This will mechanically make them more inclined to speak to you as complimenting a person is one of the exceptional techniques to get their interest, mainly if you observe it up with a question that lets in them to speak approximately themselves in element. Remember, truly all people likes a praise, and in case you anticipate a few element is more unique approximately a person these days, odds are it didn't take place thru twist of destiny and the possibility individual positioned time and effort into recognition out in that way. Noticing this validates their alternatives and will routinely make you more likeable of their eyes.

Start thru using speakme approximately some aspect they may be glaringly inquisitive about:

If you are attempting to make communique with a person but don't recognise wherein to start, a awesome desire is to in reality be observant and lead with a few component that suggests you realise some component approximately that obvious interest or hobby or are otherwise curious to recognise more. This is a high-quality manner to break the ice because of the reality it can offer you with lots to speak approximately even as at the equal time supporting you take a look at extra approximately the alternative man or woman in the way. Remember to be an lively listener on this scenario for the fine outcomes.

Lead with some aspect about your surroundings:

It doesn't depend range wherein you are; the fact which you and the opportunity character are every within the equal area at the identical time mechanically approach you have got were given have been given a few factor in not unusual. What's more, counting on in that you presently are, there are various unique similarities that might obviously shine through primarily based definitely at the proscribing elements most critical humans to the spot. Additionally, your current surroundings are a few issue that everyone goes to have an opinion on if you phrase it nicely which makes it less likely that you will get just a few phrase solution in reaction, no matter the fact that the opportunity character wasn't previously inquisitive about speakme.

Be effective to actively pay hobby due to the fact the possibility person speaks and be searching for more follow up topics to speak about whilst the conversation begins offevolved to lull.

Work to find not unusual floor:

Depending at the state of affairs that finds you and the opportunity individual together, a excellent way to find out a dependable verbal exchange problem be counted is to invite questions in desire of locating sturdy conversational floor. This manner questions on interests, famous culture, song, books and so forth are all fertile ground as all it takes is one comparable hobby to show the exploratory verbal exchange right proper into a real communique. If you do a chunk of capability probing, you in no way realize what similarities you'll possibly discover.

SOFTEN the opportunity individual up:

Regardless of what approach you are taking, there are a few nonverbal strategies you'll also need to take into account at the same time as speaking with a person new for the number one time. You need to begin by way of way of the use of Smiling on the alternative man or woman to expose that you are approachable and agreeable in preferred. Next, you will want to greet them with an Open posture to expose that you are open to new mind. Then you may need to lean in advance to ensure they understand you are interested in the communication. After that you can need to provoke physical Touch through shaking palms at the way to automatically make the opportunity individual suppose more fairly of you. Then you can to make sure you're making suitable eye contact. Finally, you will want to nod collectively with the opposite character that lets in you to preserve them absolutely talking longer.

Chapter 13: Ending A Conversation

When it consists of completing a communication properly, the maximum important trouble to do not forget is that you continuously want to have a clear time table whilst doing so. If you don't understand what you could do immediately after you've got made an effective go out from the communique, then that go out is probably wasted and alternatively the alternative person might be left with the, possibly correct, assumption that you virtually did no longer cope with their enterprise. Knowing what you will do next, may even make it tons much less complicated which will encourage yourself into motion at the same time as getting out the verbal exchange would possibly appear tough or awkward. Remember, workout makes exceptional!

Start thru finding the right 2d to bow out gracefully:

The first step to exiting a communication properly is to select the proper second to acquire this. Obviously, this acquired't be even as the modern issue remember of communication is handiest being began or at any factor while the alternative man or woman is speaking or about to speak. When the communication subsequent starts offevolved offevolved to stall, in choice to finding a new difficulty depend to speak approximately, you can begin by means of way of saying something like, "Okay," now this may every via an invitation for additonal conversation or finishing it so it is in all likelihood the other man or woman will repeat it once more questioningly. With this starting off you're then going to transport right away to the subsequent step.

Return to the start:

Next, if the conversation started out due to a selected query you requested, and that subject matter is what you have been in fact interested by, then bringing the communique decrease lower back around to that subject matter is a splendid way to get out gracefully. Use irrespective of the priority depend is as a starter after which make it clean that you will take what the opportunity person stated on the problem to coronary heart to leave a protracted-lasting impact. This is a exceptional way to cease a verbal exchange with a colleague (see chapter 10) as these conversations normally start with a specific request in mind and returning to it's miles a extremely good way to reveal you have been paying hobby as well.

Finish with the proper go out line:

Once you have delivered topics complete circle, you can need to quote a reason which you are leaving and say your goodbyes. The first problem you may want to keep in mind in this example is to be as sincere as possible, without being rude. In addition to being the right way of having out of the conversation it prevents you from having to keep in mind an complicated lie afterward.

Additionally, it's miles vital to place the emphasis on what you need to do subsequent as this could make the possibility man or woman revel in as notwithstanding the reality that they are now not the purpose you're leaving. Actions that have time sensitive additives are generally the fantastic preference because it takes the matter from your hands sincerely. Blaming a third birthday celebration is also a dependable technique. Alternatively, when you have been the only who initiated the verbal exchange then you could supply it to an stop you then definately really want to hold the word "actually" into play. For instance, "Well, I just preferred to check and ensure that..." This makes it clear which you had a easy time desk and are inquisitive about shifting on.

If the opposite party initiated the conversation to talk about some element particularly, you could outcomes get out of the communication thru asking them if there has been a few factor else you can assist with, determined by manner of a purpose you're being so direct. It is vital to no longer use this closer until then you definately definately definately have something else to do, in any other case it can seem cold.

If the above options aren't suitable, there are a few desired closers you could typically attempt to help the opportunity man or woman apprehend the conversation is at an give up. It is vital to normally use beyond disturbing language on this situation to maintain the focus wherein it desires to be. Phrases like "Anyway, it changed into tremendous to," compress the whole lot you are hoping to supply into some easy syllables. Making it easy you price the alternative character's time is also an terrific preference, as in implying that you'll permit them to get decrease again to a few thing it is they had been doing.

Chapter 14: Fake It Until You Make It

If you discover that during spite of your splendid efforts, you can't muster up the braveness to speak to strangers truly to make it less difficult for you to talk to strangers within the close to and far flung destiny; there can be one clean detail that you may do to make the whole education manner a good buy more viable. All you need to do in case you find out your self in this case is to fake it until you're making it. Specifically, you will need to fake having the confidence degree that you want you had and introduce yourself to strangers as although it modified into some thing which you did all of the time.

While this might although sound not possible, endure in mind the truth that when you have interaction with a few specific character in a confident way, even if you are without a doubt pretending to be confident, the other individual is in no manner going to understand the difference except you forestall pretending. When it involves self perception, it doesn't depend how confident you're on the interior, the give up give up result for all of us else is generally going to be the identical. What's greater, in case you faux to be assured for prolonged sufficient, some aspect first-rate will happen, you obtained't need to fake anymore and the self warranty can be actual. If this all seems like a tall story, offer it a attempt, you'll be amazed via the results.

Find a self notion function model:

When it comes to performing like you're assured, it's miles as clean as taking the time to bear in mind the person who you remember to be more self-assured than every person else you understand. With a smooth picture on your mind you'll need to then ask your self how the person in query should technique the communique you are about to have. The extra particular you will be on the subject of moves and mannerisms the better; this indicates things like body language, styles of speech and conversational behavior. Put your self into your characteristic version's headspace as virtually as possible and then do what they could do.

Approach with cause:

Those with the proper degree of self-self assurance normally tend to walk anywhere they go together with a reason. When you technique a person new, this shows you will want to accomplish that at the side of your head held lower back and your shoulders squared. If you gift your self at the equal time as slumped over and slouching you're telling the alternative character which you do not believe in your self and that they've to now not each. You might also even want to walk a bit extra speedy than everyday to suggest which you are a person who knows wherein they need to be.

Be complementary:

Self-confident humans are capable of greater with out troubles see the high-quality in the ones round them due to the truth they are acquainted with what's amazing about them as properly. This technique that drawing close to with a piece of success after which following that up via way of starting a communique with a complement and a comply with up question is a one-two punch that absolutely guarantees the alternative man or woman will keep in mind you as a person who's confident in themselves and their abilities.

Consider how beginning a communique makes you seem:

Self-assured human beings are typically taken into consideration more outstanding and outgoing than their pals. As such, in fact by way of way of manner of being the simplest to make first touch with a stranger, routinely makes them understand you as being more confident than they may be. This information must then make it even less difficult as a way to act self-assured as you are acting to an target audience that has already been glad. Taking the time to typically introduce yourself to humans you haven't met before, even in case you don't then initiate communique will allow them to apprehend which you recognise you're someone with price who deserves respect.

Speak with self perception:

When you do talk, it's far important to usually have a clean idea of what statistics you want to bring and the way you can flow into about conveying it. This will make much less difficult to be able to avoid words that the mind frequently inserts even as it's far thinking which include "like" or "uh". Additionally you'll need to make sure that you are preserving a ordinary talking tempo as speakme too quick will mean that you are nerve-racking approximately the interaction, undermining your confident façade.

www.ingramcontent.com/pod-product-compliance
Lightning Source LLC
Chambersburg PA
CBHW070557010526
44118CB00012B/1354